MERCURY READER

a custom publication

Professor Julie Jung
English 101
Illinois State University

PEARSON
Custom
Publishing

Director of Database Publishing: Michael Payne
Sponsoring Editor: Natalie Danner
Development Editors: Mary Kate Aveni and Katherine R. Gehan
Editorial Assistant: Abbey Briggs
Director of Marketing: Annabel Cellini
Operations Manager: Eric M. Kenney
Production Product Manager: Jennifer M. Berry
Rights Editor: Francesca Marcantonio
Cover Designers: Renée Sartell and Sharon Treacy

Cover Art: "Gigantia Mountains & Sea of Cortes," by R.G.K. Photography, Copyright © Tony Stone Images; "Dime," courtesy of the Shaw Collection.

Printed in the United States of America.

Please visit our websites at *www.pearsoncustom.com* and *www.mercuryreader.com*.
Attention bookstores: For permission to return any unsold stock, contact us at *pe-uscustomreturns@pearsoncustom.com*.

ISBN-13: 978-0-536-19108-3   ISBN-10: 0-536-19108-5

PEARSON CUSTOM PUBLISHING
75 Arlington St., Suite 300
Boston, MA 02116

GENERAL EDITORS

Janice Neuleib
Illinois State University

Kathleen Shine Cain
Merrimack College

Stephen Ruffus
Salt Lake Community College

Contents

VIII

⤜ REVISION ⤛

Revision is a process based on *re-seeing* an idea. An inevitable, natural part of writing, revision begins the moment a draft is finished. As you look at a draft you've completed, you find it doesn't look the way you thought it would. It *was* ideas in your head, but *now* it is sentences and paragraphs. It *was* a perfect concept, but *now* it is an imperfect piece of writing. It *was* a job you weren't sure how to do, but *now* it is started. And now the interesting work begins. Now you will find people to read the draft and give you advice. You will decide which advice you're going to act on. And you will rewrite and rewrite and rewrite.

An important preliminary to revision is getting your attitude properly adjusted. When you revise, you are not confessing your deficiencies and hoping to cover them up or be forgiven for them. You are simply looking for your assets and plotting how to take advantage of them. In the humorous play *The Importance of Being Ernest*, by Oscar Wilde, the duchess, Lady Bracknell, demonstrates the attitude you want to emulate. Lady Bracknell's son Algernon is determined to marry a pretty young woman named Cecily Cardew. At first, Lady Bracknell dismisses Cecily as a marriage prospect because the girl is a commoner. Then Lady Bracknell is told that Cecily is rich. Upon learning of Cecily's fortune, Lady Bracknell motions the young woman toward her, adjusts her spectacles and remarks, "Miss Cardew seems to me a most attractive young lady now that I look at her." The practical Lady Bracknell has adjusted her viewpoint in preparation to making the best of the situation. In the same way, a paper can change into something better before the eyes of the perceptive and flexible writer. Perhaps you have been lucky enough to have had the experience of *re-visioning* something that you have written.

While you are adjusting your attitude, you might as well double-check your concept of revision. The process of revision should not be confused with proofreading—finding a word or two used inappropriately or confusingly, or moving or removing a comma. If you do not like proofreading, we cannot blame you much, for hardly anyone does enjoy that kind of work. But proofreading is *not* revision. Nor is revision a penalty or a pointless exercise that student writers have to endure because they are in a writing class. Consider, for example, the following revision stories featuring the writers C.S. Lewis and Charles Dickens.

C.S. Lewis, author of *The Chronicles of Narnia*, and J.R.R. Tolkien, the author of *Lord of the Rings*, consulted with one another weekly on their writing, and often changed plots, characters, and themes in response to one another's suggestions as stories were developing. The two actually gave themselves life-long writing assignments by tossing a coin. Lewis's coin toss gave him the subject of space travel, and Tolkien's gave him time travel. The two worked together on these themes for most of their lives, refining and revising the original subjects.

Charles Dickens wrote his books in weekly installments in magazines. His friend, the writer Bulwer-Lytton, often made revision suggestions as the stories were appearing. Dickens also wrote an ending for "A Christmas Carol" in which Tiny Tim died! Lytton *insisted* that Dickens rewrite the story, saying that the public would never spend money on a sad ending. We can still decide whether we agree with Lytton's judgment, but he seems to have helped Dickens make considerable money in his own day.

Writers—both student and professional writers—use a variety of approaches to explore the best ways of re-seeing what they have written. Usually, revision begins with asking readers (teachers, peers, friends, or parents) to read the paper and make suggestions for substantive changes in the draft. These changes can be of several types, such as finding a new focus for the paper by changing the audience or purpose. Another possibility might be to reorganize the paper significantly to see how the parts work in a new order. Yet another way involves adding new and different materials that might change the attitude of the paper or make the information or argument considerably richer and more interesting. Some teachers ask that writers change sides of an argument and argue exactly the opposite side of a question so that the revision becomes a complete rethinking of the issues in the paper! At times, readers will suggest that the draft needs outside support or research. This new research will inevitably change the focus of the draft.

Revision can go beyond asking for advice; you can ask another writer to collaborate on the project. In business and industry, collaboration is quite common. Writers work together in teams, dividing the job, responding to one another's drafts, recombining group work in new ways, and continuing to revise and recombine until the whole project joins together as a seamless entity. Even when working teams write separately, they always come together to critique and improve one another's texts before any proposal or project is sent to a potential client. Thus, collaborative writing activities are necessary to produce both individual and collective writing for business and industry. Learning how to use another's comments for revision and learning how to be a good collaborative reader are vital to successful writing in the working world.

Since we can all read and write, we tend to think that we can all react to a writer's text easily. Actually, giving good feedback on the draft of an essay demands considerable skill and practice, not to mention intense concentration and hard work. Responding to another person's paper means doing much more than typing a kindly comment about liking the essay or scrawling a happy "good job" at the end of the draft. As you read the next section—which demonstrates drafting, commenting, and revision—pay attention to how the writer, the writer's fellow students, and the instructor contribute to the improvement of the essay, and see if you can figure out how to comment more helpfully than they did.

Taking a Paper Through the Revision Process

What follows is a model of a student paper in three separate drafts, annotated with comments from the instructor and fellow students. Watch carefully how the essay changes as a result of the input received, how that input does or does not agree with your own, and how successful you think the final draft is.

The student, Tom, has been asked by his instructor to respond to a cultural icon (an ad, a TV show, a music video, a sports star, etc.) and evaluate the icon chosen. Tom chooses to write about a Bacardi Rum ad. Tom was given the assignment to write a persuasive paper examining that cultural icon, making sure to include how it uses ethos (does the ad show authority?) and pathos (is the intended audience of the ad moved or persuaded to buy the product as a result of viewing the ad?).

Draft 1 _____

[In carrying out the assignment, Tom looks at the ad, describes it, and writes down his perceptions pretty much in the order that they occur to him. By the time he has finished, Tom has figured out what he thinks about the ad, so the draft is a *record* of his thought process. As you will see, this strategy helps Tom as a writer; he gets his ideas down, but the draft quickly confuses readers, who expect Tom to get to the point. Beginning with the second paragraph, Tom's student readers grow confused and suggest various additions and reorganizations to create a more coherent piece of writing. Feel free to write your own comments next to those that Tom's readers have already provided.]

_____

Why Buy Bacardi Rum

¶1 The image of an old, dark gothic apartment building stands silent and abandoned on a city street on a brisk fall day. For just one moment using your imagination you take a bottle and add a shimmering splash of clear Puerto Rican Rum to the setting, turning the gray and black concrete exterior of the building to fresh tropical colors of pastel blue and pink. The once bare and gaunt birch tree in front of the old apartment is suddenly transformed into a tall tropical palm tree blowing in a calm ocean breeze. The images and theme of this situation are found in the new advertisement for rum. The idea is very imaginative and abstract, yet its message is clear, "Just add Bacardi Rum."

¶2 The headline "Just Add Bacardi Rum" is imposed on a clear blue sky, in vibrant green and pink, above the once glum apartment. This statement implies that it is simple or easy to add a little excitement to a situation and indirectly says drinking rum can brighten or improve your social and party life.

¶3 This advertisement applies to anyone...anyone of the drinking age of course. Many brands of hard alcohol try to carry an image associated with the type of alcohol and its origin. Most Rum ads try to capture the image as authentic and pure. This is very effective. Along with this, I believe many advertisements for alcohol use a great deal of imaginative ideas, to in essence, ignore some of the effects that actually do go along with drinking. Rum producers know that everyone is interested in a change for the better. It may be a change for something warmer, brighter, or more fun. Bacardi feels that they can offer this change. This rum ad grasps the audience's imagination and also uses factual information and logic to establish credibility in order to persuade consumers.

¶4 After the initial perception of the advertisement's main theme, your attention is drawn to the side margin of the advertisement where there is a smaller title or headline declaring "The World's Great Rum. Made in Puerto Rico." Many types of alcohol are associated with different regions in the world and the people that live there. For instance, Russian vodka, Mexican tequila, and Scottish whiskey. These associations with the type of alcohol and the country in which they are produced hold very strong in the mind of the consumers, and many good relations are made with respect to the quality.

> *Student Comment: Move these last two sentences back to paragraph three?*

Underneath this headline it is logically explained that the world's finest rum has been made in Puerto Rico for over 400 years, and that rum is actually made at a distillery in San Juan, Puerto Rico. This is a great logical approach to prove to the consumer that this rum actually is "The World's Great Rum."

> *Student Comment: The proof is not clear here.*

The ethos of the advertisement is then further established because the advertisement encourages you to actually come to the distillery in San Juan and take a tour and see for yourself the quality and craftsmanship that go into the creation of their product. This shows that the company themselves have a great amount of trust and assurance in their product. *Quality* and *craftsmanship* are two very good characterizing words that make the audience for this ad gain trust for the company's product. Furthermore, in the margin and on the bottle the company insignia looks very classic and authentic, and it is confirmed that Bacardi was established in 1862, which proves that the name is time-honored. These are very strong arguments that logically prove that the company is credible and trustworthy.

Student Comment: The paragraph confuses ethos and pathos. Suggest you organize your ideas around either ethos or pathos in the paragraph. It would make the paper much easier to follow.

¶5 The main theme of this advertisement is very appealing to the audience's imagination. The main "visual" of the advertisement is an abstract and imaginative picture as you saw by the opening description. The bright images in the ad such as the sparkling rum and the exotic Puerto Rican palm tree demand attention and pull the audience's imagination into the ad. The "visual" of a new bright apartment and a palm tree glistening in the sun compared to the original picture, before the splash of rum, of an old worn-down apartment is much more appealing. Associations that the audience may make with an old worn-down gothic apartment may be ideas such as uninviting, boredom, and dullness. These are some of the associations that many people may relate to their everyday boring lives.

Student Comment: Why wasn't this point made in the first paragraph?

On the other hand, the associations that many people make with respect to palm trees, pastel colors, and glistening tropical rum are much more positive and inviting. Delusions of vacation, the Caribbean, excitement, and refreshing tropical drinks dance through the audience's subconscious. This could be looked at as escapism. According to the ad, the transition from boring to exciting is directly a result of Bacardi. This leaves a very black and white impression on the audience.

Student Comment: The last sentence does not seem to follow the one before it.

Pathos is used very effectively in this advertisement by capturing the audience's imagination.

¶6 Everyone is interested in a change for the better. This rum takes this idea and achieves the original theme that they set out to create by using an innovative, clever idea. Their argument is furthered by the use of credibility and logic. In one sentence, I believe Bacardi is claiming just this: if you are leading an uninteresting, plain life and you are interested in making a transition for the better, "Just Add Bacardi Rum," the world's great drink that is made in Puerto Rico.

End of First Draft _____

Peer Review

Because it is important (and always more effective) to elicit feedback on a draft, asking specific questions that arise in the writer's mind as the piece is written, Tom asks his readers:

I describe only one ad. Does this weaken my argument? What other argument could I have added?

> *Student Comment: It may weaken your argument. I think it could be stronger if you found another similar ad for more ideas. You describe ideas from the ad but never tell why or how they would affect people.*

> *Student Comment: I never saw a clear argument being established. If I had to guess what your argument was, I would say you approved of Bacardi's ad, but even that is hard to pull out.*

Any draft of any paper can evoke different responses from multiple readers. That is why we ask more than one person to read a paper, but the responses here seem to be fairly consistent—that the paper is somewhat jumbled and that the argument of the paper is hard to discover. In the original assignment, the teacher has clearly asked for an analysis of ethos and pathos. The writer, Tom, has tried to use those words without quite understanding how to explain his ideas.

Draft 2 _____

[Note that the second draft is easier to follow because Tom has moved some sentences around and provided some transitional material to help keep the readers on track. You will see that the readers make fewer global comments such as "I got lost." Since Tom is starting to make the point clearer, the readers begin to focus on smaller details. The second paragraph still has some significant problems with clarity, mainly because Tom is still unwilling to state his argumentative thesis there.]

_____

Why Buy Bacardi Rum

¶1 The image of an old, dark gothic apartment building stands silent and abandoned on a city street on a brisk fall day. For just one moment using your imagination you take a bottle and add a shimmering splash of clear Bacardi Puerto Rican Rum to the setting, turning the gray and black concrete exterior of the building to fresh tropical colors of pastel blue and pink. The once bare and gaunt birch tree in front of the old apartment is suddenly transformed into a tall tropical palm tree blowing in a calm ocean breeze. The images and theme of this situation are found in the new advertisement for Puerto Rican Rum. The idea is very imaginative and abstract, yet its message is clear, "Just Add Bacardi Rum."

¶2 The headline "Just Add Bacardi Rum" is imposed on a clear blue sky in vibrant green and pink, above the once glum apartment This statement implies that it is simple or easy to add a little excitement to a situation and indirectly says drinking rum can brighten or improve your social and party life (or any situation). (*Tom added the last three words, but otherwise left the first two paragraphs untouched*).

¶3 (*Major changes appear at this point* :) How do hard alcohol manufacturers sell their products? (*new sentence*) Many types of hard alcohol (*new word*) are associated with the type of alcohol and its origin. Many types of alcohol are associated with (*new words*) different regions in the world and the people that live there. For instance, Russian vodka, Mexican tequila, and Scottish whiskey. These associations with the type of alcohol and the country in which they are produced hold very strong in the mind of the consumers, and many good relations are made with respect to the quality. (*The readers here had suggested moving the preceding two sentences, which had been in paragraph four in draft 1 back to this paragraph, and Tom chose to follow that suggestion.*) (*Notice the cutting of two sentences here from draft 1 in response to the reader's suggestions.*) Most rum ads try to capture the image as authentic and pure. This is very effective. Along with this, I believe many advertisements for alcohol use a great deal of imaginative ideas, to in essence, ignore some of the effects that actually do go along with drinking. This is easily seen in the description of the rum ad (*new sentence*). This advertisement can apply to anyone...anyone of the drinking age of course. (*One student reader had suggested moving what had been sentence one in paragraph three in the first draft to this point, and Tom chose to do that.*) Rum producers know that everyone is interested in a change for the better. It may be a change for something warmer, brighter, or more fun. The distributors feel that they can offer this change. This rum ad accomplishes this by grasping (*changed wording*) the audience's imagination with a colorful "visual" (*phrase added*) and also uses factual information and logic to establish credibility in order to persuade consumers.

᠁ Revision ᠁

Editor's Note—One reader had written in the margin of the first draft "too many ideas in this paragraph." Tom did not decrease the number of ideas, but did choose to move the sentences suggested.

¶4 Logic and credibility reinforce the ad (*new sentence meant to provide the transition asked for by one student reader*). After the initial perception of the advertisement's main theme, "Just Add Bacardi Rum," (*repetition added*) your attention is drawn to the side margin of the advertisement where there is a smaller title or headline declaring "The World's Great Rum. Made in Puerto Rico." Underneath this headline it is logically explained that the world's finest rum has been made in Puerto Rico for over 400 years, and that Bacardi Rum is actually made at a distillery in San Juan, Puerto Rico. This is a great logical approach to prove to the consumer Bacardi Rum actually is "The World's Great Rum." (*In the first draft, a student reader noted that the proof here was not clear.*) The ethos of the advertisement is then further established because the advertisement encourages you to actually come to the distillery in San Juan and take a tour and see for yourself the quality and craftsmanship that go into the creation of their product. This shows that the company themselves have a great amount of trust and assurance in their product. *Quality* and *craftsmanship* are two very good characterizing words that make the audience for this ad gain trust for the company's product. Furthermore, in the margin and on the bottle the company insignia looks very classic and authentic, and it is confirmed that Bacardi was established in 1862, which proves that the name is time-honored. These are very strong arguments that logically prove that the company is credible and trustworthy.

> *Instructor Comment: This paragraph is the strongest point of your analysis, but how does it tie into the thesis? Also, how does Bacardi differ from other rums?*

Editor's Note—The student questions about this paragraph seem to have been ignored.

¶5 The main theme of this advertisement is very appealing to the audience's imagination. The main "visual" of the advertisement is an abstract and imaginative picture as you saw by the opening description. The bright images in the ad such as the sparkling rum and the exotic Puerto Rican palm tree demand attention and pull the audience's imagination into the ad. The visual of a new bright apartment and a palm tree glistening in the sun compared to the original picture, before the splash of rum, of an old worn-down apartment is much more appealing. Associations that the audience may make with an old worn-down gothic apartment may be ideas such as uninviting, boredom, and dullness. These are some of the associations that many people may relate to their everyday boring lives.

> *Student Comment: Why wasn't this point made in the first paragraph?*

On the other hand, the associations that many people make with respect to palm trees, pastel colors, and glistening tropical rum are much more positive and inviting. Delusions of vacation, the Caribbean, excitement, and refreshing tropical drinks dance through the audience's subconscious. This could be looked at as escapism. According to the ad, the transition from boring to exciting is directly a result of rum. This leaves a very black and white impression on the audience.

> *Student Comment: The last sentence does not seem to follow the one before it.*

Just add rum if you want a change for the better. Pathos is used very effectively in this advertisement by capturing the audience's imagination (*sentence added*).

¶6 Everyone is interested in a change for the better. This ad claims, "Just Add Bacardi Rum (for a change for the better)." The distributor takes this idea and achieves the original theme that they set out to create by using an innovative, clever idea (*sentence added*). Their argument is furthered by the use of credibility and logic. In one sentence, I believe the producer is claiming just this: if you are leading an uninteresting, plain life and you are interested in making a transition for the better, "Just Add Bacardi Rum," the world's great drink that is made in Puerto Rico.

End of Second Draft _____

Teacher/ Student Conversation

The teacher commented: "I think your analysis is one of the strongest aspects of your paper. I can see the work you are doing on transitions and am truly impressed with all the work you are doing with voice. I think I understand your decision to hold your thesis off until the end of your paper, but I have concerns similar to your own. Would it be better to work your thesis in earlier? Would it make your argument stronger?"

Tom wrote back: "At times in my writing process, I wondered if possibly I was over-analyzing, but I came to realize that everything in an ad is put there for a reason. One weakness in my paper may be that I used only one ad, but that made it much easier to go into depth on the one ad that I did use. I believe the single strongest parts of my paper are my descriptions. I think the weakest part may still be my organization. I put the thesis at the end so that I could illustrate my point with the descriptions, but it may have weakened the paper since some of my fellow students felt they were reading aimlessly. I moved the suggested sentences to try to help these readers see where the paper was going.

Tom's first two drafts illustrate the process of revision. The writer writes; a fellow writer, acting as critical reader, responds. The teacher could be considered the editor in the case of a classroom situation and does not enter the conversation until the second draft. The writer then makes changes according to his or her best judgment. Then the readers and instructor respond once again, usually with more extensive written comments. More revision could follow as long as the writer and readers want to continue to improve the paper. There is no magic number of revisions!

Tom's paper still has several problems that have not been addressed. His late-appearing thesis may be related to his lack of a clear audience. He reasons about the ad, but he does not seem quite to know what he wants his readers to think or do. Should they buy the rum? Should they write to the TV station to object to the ad? Should they try to see the ad on television to enjoy the clever way that it is produced? The reader is still left with questions about the purpose of the paper. So far, Tom has a free-standing analysis that is in itself interesting but does not quite draw an audience into his thinking. He has confused the ethos of the rum ad writers with his own need for ethos. We now know what the appeal of the rum ad is, but we still cannot quite figure out what the appeal of Tom's analysis is. Regardless of these concerns, it is still important to note that considerable progress has been made in the second draft.

Draft 3 _____

[Notice in draft three that Tom does more real revision than in either of the other two drafts: he decides on a lot of cutting and he rearranges whole paragraphs. He can make these changes because he has finally decided to make his main point clear in the second paragraph. Once he focuses on explaining how the ad uses imagination and information to create the appeals of pathos and logos, he can throw out the information he does not need to support his thesis, and he can rearrange the rest of the information to create a more successful piece of writing.]

_____

"Why Buy Bacardi Rum?"

¶1 The image of an old, dark gothic apartment building stands silent and abandoned on a city street on a brisk fall day. For just one moment using your imagination you take a bottle and add a shimmering splash of clear Bacardi Puerto Rican Rum to the setting, turning the gray and black concrete exterior of the building to fresh tropical colors of pastel blue and pink. The once stale, bare, and gaunt birch tree in front of the old apartment is suddenly transformed into a tall tropical palm tree blowing in a calm ocean breeze. (*Notice that two sentences were removed here and replaced with the following sentence.*) This new Bacardi Rum ad appeals to the audience's imagination. (*The following sentences are the former paragraph five.*) The main "visual" of the advertisement is abstract and imaginative, with bright images of the sparkling rum and the exotic Puerto Rican palm. The new bright apartment and palm tree glistening in the sun beckon the audience away from the old worn-down gothic apartment that suggested boredom and dullness of everyday life (*the wording has been condensed in this sentence*). On the other hand, many people find palm trees, pastel colors, and glistening tropical rum much more positive and inviting. Images of a Caribbean vacation with excitement and refreshing tropical drinks dance through the audience's imagination. According to the ad, the transition from boring to exciting results directly from pouring Bacardi Rum. (*A sentence was cut, followed by an added sentence.*) Just add rum if you want a change for the better. This argument uses pathos very effectively by capturing the audience's imagination (*no new paragraph here now*). The headline "Just Add Bacardi Rum" implies that it is simple or easy to add a little excitement to a situation and indirectly says drinking rum can brighten or improve your social and party life (*or any situation*).

¶2 (*formerly paragraph 3*) How do hard liquor (*note the change in words from* alcohol *to* liquor) manufacturers sell their products? Many types of hard liquor are associated with the regions in the world where they are made and with the people who live in those regions. For instance, Russian vodka, Mexican tequila, and Scottish whiskey. These associations are positive and pleasing to most buyers and consumers (*notice the cut and the substitution here*). Most rum ads try to capture this local image, because it presents the liquor (*added phrase*) as authentic and pure. This is very effective because the advertisers want the buyer to ignore some of the effects that actually do go along with drinking (*notice the cuts*). (*Two sentences cut.*) Rum producers want buyers to ignore the negatives (*added*). They also know that everyone is interested in a change for the better. It may be a change for something warmer, brighter, or more fun. The rum producers feel that they can offer this change. This rum ad accomplishes this end by grasping the audience's imagination with a colorful "visual" and uses factual information and logic to establish credibility in order to persuade consumers.

¶3 Logic and credibility reinforce the ad. After the initial perception of the advertisement's main theme, "Just Add Bacardi Rum," your attention is drawn to the side margin of the advertisement where there is a smaller title or headline declaring "The World's Great Rum. Made in Puerto Rico."

¶4 (*New paragraph*) Underneath this headline, advertisers say that the world's finest rum has been made in Puerto Rico for over 400 years, and that Bacardi Puerto Rican Rum is actually made at a distillery in San Juan, Puerto Rico. This is a great logical approach to prove the authenticity (*added phrase*) of the rum to the consumer and to prove that the rum actually (*added phrase*) is "The World's Great Rum." The advertisement encourages the viewers (*added word*) to come to the distillery in San Juan and take a tour and see for themselves (*added word*) the quality and craftsmanship that go into the creation of their product. This shows that the company themselves (*notice the cuts*) guarantee (*word added*) their product. Quality and craftsmanship (*notice the cuts*) characterize the company's product (*notice the cuts*). Furthermore, in the margin and on the bottle the company insignia looks very classic and authentic, and (*cuts*) confirms that Bacardi was established in 1862, proving that the name is time-honored. These are very strong arguments that logically prove that the company is credible and trustworthy. Bacardi is clearly the oldest and the best rum on the market according to this ad's argument (*added*).

¶5 (This has been moved to paragraph one.)

¶6 Everyone is interested in a change for the better. The distributor has taken this idea and achieved the original theme (*notice the cuts*) by using an innovative and clever idea. (*Notice the cut sentence.*) In one sentence, the producer is claiming just this: if you are leading an uninteresting, plain life and you are interested in making a transition for the better, "Just Add Bacardi Rum" the world's greatest Puerto Rican rum.

End of Third Draft _____

Tom has polished the copy and has strengthened the whole analysis by moving his thesis to the beginning, as his readers had suggested. He has also made the language smoother and more flowing and illustrated the power of the ad's logic rather than just *saying* that the ad had logic on its side.

Ongoing Revision

The important point to understand about revision is that it is never finished. In a class situation, the end of the semester ends revision, as it did for Tom, but in an ideal situation, this paper might reappear as a source for a new idea or an extended paper in another context. For example, Tom might take an advanced writing course in which he would decide to turn the paper into a study of how ads are aimed at influencing the behavior of young people. He might look at addictive substances like cigarettes to discover how those ads target young prospective users. He might do research into the ad industry to discover how marketers work to target an audience. He might also want to target a particular audience himself, perhaps writing a draft of this paper that would urge young readers to notice when an ad is appealing to their better interests and when it is appealing only to their self-indulgence or need to belong.

The important point to note from reading the three drafts of Tom's paper, along with his peer readers' responses and his teacher's reactions, is that he listened to the advice of his readers and made noticeable changes, and that he also entered into a conversation with his teacher about the changes he had made and would make in later drafts. The most important value a writer can adopt is the value of his or her ownership of any draft. The changes belong to the writer; the responsibility for good reading and good suggestions lies with the peer readers and the teacher.

THE MAKER'S EYE: REVISING YOUR OWN MANUSCRIPTS

Donald M. Murray

Donald M. Murray (1924–2006), born in Boston, spent most of his life writing, editing, and teaching writing. He published fiction, poetry, and a variety of nonfiction. He was an editor for Time *magazine and in 1954 won a Pulitzer Prize for editorial writing. His textbooks on writing include* Writing for Your Readers, A Writer Teaches Writing, Write to Learn, Read to Write, *and* The Craft of Revision. *The following essay was published in the journal* The Writer *in 1973. As you read about how Murray approached revision, think about your own writing and revising habits.*

When students complete a first draft, they consider the job of writing done—and their teachers too often agree. When professional writers complete a first draft, they usually feel that they are at the start of the writing process. When a draft is completed, the job of writing can begin.

That difference in attitude is the difference between amateur and professional, inexperience and experience, journeyman and craftsman. Peter F. Drucker, the prolific business writer, calls his first draft "the zero draft"—after that he can start counting. Most writers share the feeling that the first draft, and all of those which follow, are opportunities to discover what they have to say and how best they can say it.

To produce a progression of drafts, each of which says more and says it more clearly, the writer has to develop a special kind of reading skill. In school we are taught to decode what appears on the page as finished writing. Writers, however, face a different category of possibility and responsibility when they read their own drafts. To them the words on the page are never finished. Each can be changed and rearranged, can set off a chain reaction of confusion or clarified meaning. This is a different kind of reading, which is possibly more difficult and certainly more exciting.

Writers must learn to be their own best enemy. They must accept the criticism of others and be suspicious of it; they must accept the praise of others and be even more suspicious of it. Writers cannot depend on others. They must detach themselves from their own pages so that they can apply both their caring and their craft to their own work.

5   Such detachment is not easy. Science fiction writer Ray Bradbury   5
supposedly puts each manuscript away for a year to the day and then rereads it as a stranger. Not many writers have the discipline or the time to do this. We must read when our judgment may be at its worst, when we are close to the euphoric moment of creation.

Then the writer, counsels novelist Nancy Hale, "should be critical of everything that seems to him most delightful in his style. He should excise what he most admires, because he wouldn't thus admire it if he weren't . . . in a sense protecting it from criticism." John Ciardi, the poet, adds, "The last act of the writing must be to become one's own reader. It is, I suppose, a schizophrenic process, to begin passionately and to end critically, to begin hot and to end cold; and, more important, to be passion-hot and critic-cold at the same time."

Most people think that the principal problem is that writers are too proud of what they have written. Actually, a greater problem for most professional writers is one shared by the majority of students. They are overly critical, think everything is dreadful, tear up page after page, never complete a draft, see the task as hopeless.

The writer must learn to read critically but constructively, to cut what is bad, to reveal what is good. Eleanor Estes, the children's book author, explains: "The writer must survey his work critically, coolly, as though he were a stranger to it. He must be willing to prune, expertly and hard-heartedly. At the end of each revision, a manuscript may look . . . worked over, torn apart, pinned together, added to, deleted from, words changed and words changed back. Yet the book must maintain its original freshness and spontaneity."

Most readers underestimate the amount of rewriting it usually takes to produce spontaneous reading. This is a great disadvantage to the student writer, who sees only a finished product and never watches the craftsman who takes the necessary step back, studies the work carefully, returns to the task, steps back, returns, steps back, again and again. Anthony Burgess, one of the most prolific writers in the English-speaking world, admits, "I might revise a page twenty times." Roald Dahl, the popular children's writer, states, "By the time I'm nearing the end of a story, the first part will have been reread and altered and corrected at least 150 times. . . . Good writing is essentially rewriting. I am positive of this."

10   Rewriting isn't virtuous. It isn't something that ought to be done. It is simply something that most writers find they have to do to discover what they have to say and how to say it. It is a condition of the writer's life.

There are, however, a few writers who do little formal rewriting, primarily because they have the capacity and experience to create and review a large number of invisible drafts in their minds before they approach the page. And some writers slowly produce finished pages, performing all the tasks of revision simultaneously, page by page, rather than draft by draft. But it is still possible to see the sequence followed by most writers most of the time in rereading their own work.

Most writers scan their drafts first, reading as quickly as possible to catch the larger problems of subject and form, then move in closer and closer as they read and write, reread and rewrite.

The first thing writers look for in their drafts is information. They know that a good piece of writing is built from specific, accurate, and interesting information. The writer must have an abundance of information from which to construct a readable piece of writing.

Next writers look for *meaning* in the information. The specifics must build a pattern of significance. Each piece of specific information must carry the reader toward meaning.

15   Writers reading their own drafts are aware of *audience*. They put themselves in the reader's situation and make sure that they deliver information which a reader wants to know or needs to know in a manner which is easily digested. Writers try to be sure that they anticipate and answer the questions a critical reader will ask when reading the piece of writing.

Writers make sure that the *form* is appropriate to the subject and the audience. Form, or genre, is the vehicle which carries meaning to the reader, but form cannot be selected until the writer has adequate information to discover its significance and an audience which needs or wants that meaning.

Once writers are sure the form is appropriate, they must then look at the *structure,* the order of what they have written. Good writing is built on a solid framework of logic, argument, narrative, or motivation which runs through the entire piece of writing and holds it together. This is the time when many writers find it most effective to outline as a way of visualizing the hidden spine by which the piece of writing is supported.

The element on which writers may spend a majority of their time is *development.* Each section of a piece of writing must be adequately developed. It must give readers enough information so that they are satisfied. How much information is enough? That's as difficult as asking how much garlic belongs in a salad. It must be done to taste, but most beginning writers underdevelop, underestimating the reader's hunger for information.

As writers solve development problems, they often have to consider questions of *dimension.* There must be a pleasing and effective proportion among all the parts of the piece of writing. There is a continual process of subtracting and adding to keep the piece of writing in balance.

20 Finally, writers have to listen to their own voices. *Voice* is the force 20 which drives a piece of writing forward. It is an expression of the writer's authority and concern. It is what is between the words on the page, what glues the piece of writing together. A good piece of writing is always marked by a consistent, individual voice.

As writers read and reread, write and rewrite, they move closer and closer to the page until they are doing line-by-line editing. Writers read their own pages with infinite care. Each sentence, each line, each clause, each phrase, each word, each mark of punctuation, each section of white space between the type has to contribute to the clarification of meaning.

Slowly the writer moves from word to word, looking through language to see the subject. As a word is changed, cut, or added, as a construction is rearranged, all the words used before that moment and all those that follow that moment must be considered and reconsidered.

Writers often read aloud at this stage of the editing process, muttering or whispering to themselves, calling on the ear's experience with language. Does this sound right—or that? Writers edit, shifting back and forth from eye to page to ear to page. I find I must do this careful editing in short runs, no more than fifteen or twenty minutes at a stretch, or I become too kind with myself. I begin to see what I hope is on the page, not what actually is on the page.

This sounds tedious if you haven't done it, but actually it is fun. Making something right is immensely satisfying, for writers begin to learn what they are writing about by writing. Language leads them to meaning, and there is the joy of discovery, of understanding, of making meaning clear as the writer employs the technical skills of language.

25   Words have double meanings, even triple and quadruple meanings. Each word has its own potential for connotation and denotation. And when writers rub one word against the other, they are often rewarded with a sudden insight, an unexpected clarification.

The maker's eye moves back and forth from word to phrase to sentence to paragraph to sentence to phrase to word. The maker's eye sees the need for variety and balance, for a firmer structure, for a more appropriate form. It peers into the interior of the paragraph, looking for coherence, unity, and emphasis, which make meaning clear.

I learned something about this process when my first bifocals were prescribed. I had ordered a larger section of the reading portion of the glass because of my work, but even so, I could not contain my eyes within this new limit of vision. And I still find myself taking off my glasses and bending my nose towards the page, for my eyes unconsciously flick back and forth across the page, back to another page, forward to still another, as I try to see each evolving line in relation to every other line.

When does this process end? Most writers agree with the great Russian writer Tolstoy, who said, "I scarcely ever reread my published writings, if by chance I come across a page, it always strikes me: all this must be rewritten; this is how I should have written it."

The maker's eye is never satisfied, for each word has the potential to ignite new meaning. This article has been twice written all the way through the writing process, and it was published four years ago. Now it is to be republished in a book. The editors make a few small suggestions, and then I read it with my maker's eye. Now it has been re-edited, re-revised, re-read, re-re-edited, for each piece of writing to the writer is full of potential and alternatives.

30   A piece of writing is never finished. It is delivered to a deadline, torn out of the typewriter on demand, sent off with a sense of accomplishment and shame and pride and frustration. If only there were a couple more days, time for just another run at it, perhaps then . . .

Questions on Meaning

1. Why should writers be suspicious of the criticism of others and even more suspicious of the praise of others?
2. Explain why and how rewriting is an opportunity for writers "to discover what they have to say." Why don't, or can't, writers know in advance what they want to say?

Questions on Rhetorical Strategy and Style

1. Describe the essay's thesis in your own words. Does Murray express it in one statement anywhere in the essay?
2. How does Murray analyze the process of rewriting? Is there one set process all writers go through, with steps in the same order, or does it vary? Describe this process fully.
3. Murray defines eight specific elements of writing that the writer examines and works on in the rewriting process. List these and define each in our own words.
4. Murray quotes a number of different writers on how they go about rewriting. The use of these quotations involves which of the eight elements?

Writing Assignments

1. Search your belongings for any piece of writing you did long ago—a letter, a school paper, anything. Read it and critique it objectively. What are its strengths? What would you want to rewrite now? How do you see it differently now from when you wrote it?
2. Write an essay in which you describe your own rewriting process—the method you use when you don't "have to" rewrite as part of an assignment. Be honest with yourself about how you actually work, and discuss what constraints of time and other factors affect your process. Analyze the strengths and weaknesses of your approach to rewriting.

WRITING ABOUT VISUAL TEXTS

Visual Literacy: Why Is It Important?

It seems obvious to say that we live in an age of mass media and that visual forms of communication are dominant. Therefore, it seems more than speculative to suggest that since we are constantly exposed to mass media, the visual must have a profound influence on our lives. The operative term here is *media,* as in *mediated.* Our understanding of the world is, to a significant extent, influenced by the entities that produce the imagery we consume. We accept this belief more readily than we might be aware. For example, many public schools across the nation have dress code requirements against wearing clothing that displays logos, or t-shirts with political statements. This example illustrates how people accept that images influence behavior and social relations. Understanding visual forms is a high-stakes matter in the twenty-first century and they reveal much about how people define themselves and relate to others.

Visual images, whether they are cartoons, photos, advertisements, charts, graphs, reproductions of art, or documents, all demand a slightly different kind of thought processing than the process of reading written text, such as an essay, poem, or a piece of fiction. An image by its nature is meant to evoke different kinds of logical and emotional reactions. When we see a picture or icon we immediately activate the center of our brains where our emotional reactions take place. Almost instantly, we prepare to laugh or get mad or be sad. That's why the funnies in the newspaper so quickly grab most people's attention. The reasoning parts of the brain get a short circuit because the feeling parts of the brain have kicked in with a response.

Analyzing the Immediate Response

This reaction can be good or bad, but most often the power of the response tops anything that we get from a prose or even a poetry passage simply because the reaction happens so quickly. An image of war engages our feelings whatever they may be: patriotism, repulsion, even excitement. A cartoon about the challenges of writing reminds us how we feel when we set out to write something, not of how our brains struggle to come up with a new idea.

Courtesy of the Corbis Corporation.

These emotional explosions help to evoke topics for writing, but they also can make us to stop and do the logical work, too. Take the example of an image of war, such as the famous WWII photograph of the Marines raising the American flag at Iwo Jima. After the first emotional hit from the image, we have to stop and analyze the emotion. What caused the reaction? What was it about the image that brought up the particular reaction? What can we then say about both the feeling and the analysis of the feeling? How do we get from the feeling to a topic that will be worth writing about and, more importantly, that will be worth a reader's time?

The first question about the cause of the reaction can be the key to the analysis and to the writer's topic. A powerful reaction to an image tells us that this image has something to do with an issue that matters to us. If the war image recalls stories told by a relative who fought in a war, then the topic might be about that historical memoir and the events surrounding it. The war image can evoke powerful political feelings about an upcoming election, a recent military campaign, or social issues relating to the image. Politics can become the topic of the writing. We react to images because they connect with something we know and care about, so we can in turn produce a topic based on that connection.

Associations with the Image

Questions for writing that follow the images often ask for associations that will lead from the image to a related topic. Use questions to help you make these associations. To return to the war example, a question might be about why you associate the war image with a history course you have taken, or with something you have read, or a movie you have seen. What do you know about the battle for Iwo Jima and how do you know it? How much do you know about the specific circumstances surround the taking of the photograph? For example, were you aware that the photograph was composed, not spontaneous? What effect did this photograph have on the war effort? This kind of association can even lead you to further research as you begin to connect the image with other experiences you have had both in school and in society. The trick is to use the associative questions to free up your own knowledge base and your own background. In that way, you can use the image and the question to help you make the paper you write your own.

Cartoon images help to associate ideas as well as other images. For example, cartoons on writing, such as Charles Schultz's the Peanuts cartoon of Snoopy writing a novel, remind each of us of papers we wrote and writing classes we had. Such a cartoon reminds us that writing is a struggle with one's own identity and desire to achieve meaning. This cartoon itself, or the questions following it, can help you to write your own authorial autobiography. What have you written, and who gave you the idea for the writing? Who are you as a writer? Do you struggle like the cartoon writer? What's easy to write, and what's hard? These associations can help you to write about yourself as a writer, and to discover topics in your own writing history. Many writers return to the same paper or topic over and over again, reworking a theme in different ways over a lifetime.

Talking with Others

Don't count only on your own reaction. Be sure to ask others about their reactions to the image. Writing happens best in interactive situations, so take advantage of the class and of other people you know so that you can get as many reactions as possible. The image may affect a friend quite differently than it affects you, so you will have at least two different readings of the image to work with as you develop your ideas. Also, others might read an image very differently than you do and might give you another interpretation that changes what you were planning to say. This process can continue as you write about the image. Keep double-checking against your own first reaction because that too can change as you think more about what you want to say. You can be your own "other."

Group work is important in all writing because you need the group's reactions to enrich what you are doing. A discussion among three or four people can evoke new ideas that one person alone could not have come up with; otherwise there would be no point in most of the brainstorming sessions that take place. A group does work that an individual cannot do alone. Keep in mind as you talk to your group about the image that the group might be going in new directions, and be open to those new directions.

Comparisons and Contrasts

Don't limit yourself to the image at hand. Especially with business or science charts and graphs, look for more images that will help you to understand the concept you are shaping. Even with pictures and drawings, don't hesitate to find more images that will enrich the one you first responded to and used to trigger your topic. For example, your war image might lead you to books or Web sites that give more information and more images about the first visual. Use the expanded visions to elaborate on your ideas, or use the added data to help you understand or complicate your first idea.

If the first reaction to an image is emotional, the later reactions can be puzzlement or curiosity. Added data in the form of more images can help to resolve the puzzlement or to complicate it in new ways. Satisfying curiosity about the person who took the picture or drew the image can also enrich your understanding. Where was the photographer when the picture was taken? What relationship did the artist have to the picture? Knowledge of other photos or pictures can enrich your understanding and tell you why the image was chosen.

Remember to keep your curiosity working as you write about the image. If it reminds you of another image that is similar or different, find out why. Use the associations to enrich your text, and continue to follow this kind of thinking as you work. It is important to trust this impulse to connect ideas so that you will produce a piece of writing that will evoke responses in readers and increase their interest with their own associations and comparisons.

Finding an Audience

Writing about visuals can often lead to the kinds of discovery writing described here, but finally most of us use our writing to find readers who share the interests and curiosity that we expressed. That can mean that you will have to rethink your first drafts of your writing. For example, back to the war image, how can you find an appropriate reader for your writing? It doesn't do to say, "someone who is interested in war." The scope is too wide. Let's assume that you have discovered that the image was taken during the Vietnam war and that you responded because you had an uncle in that war. You write about the uncle's experiences and about his struggles after the war. You decide that the essay might interest other war veterans or others who have family in the military now. You may find that the essay can be focused for a magazine that appeals to the military or even to a newsmagazine. In either case, taking time to consider the audience will help to improve your essay about visuals, and give it a purpose.

Visual Texts as Rhetorical

Why would we apply the term "text" to an image? Ordinarily, when we think of a text, we think of something in print. However, our notion of the text has expanded due to an interest in the significance of visual mediums in our lives. So much about our understanding of the world around us is represented visually. In fact, even printed texts accomplish something by virtue of their visual components. Texts now employ far more visual characteristics because of society's appetite and need for visual appeal. An image, or visual text, whether it is a photograph or cartoon, was created by someone to influence how the viewer will see it. In fact, today many people think of, say, an advertisement as a visual essay, as having a type of grammar and syntax of its own. Now we have become used to the idea of *reading* images. Therefore, thinking of an image as a *text* and thinking of its creator/artist as the *author* is helpful in developing an interpretive stance toward it. It is also helpful to understand the conventions of the given image and consider how those conventions have been deployed and for a given purpose. For example, the Iwo Jima photograph uses light and shadow in many ways to convey its meanings. It frames the subjects (the soldiers, the flag) in a particular manner, that is, the photographer chooses what to include and how to include elements in the frame for an intended rhetorical effect. In short, to better appreciate the rhetorical nature of all texts, including visual texts, you might ask yourself questions such as the following:

- What issue motivated the author of the image?
- What is the author's primary purpose?
- How does the image's arrangement convey its purpose and message?
- What response is he or she trying to provoke in viewers?
- Why did the author choose the particular medium?
- How does the image conform (or not) to the conventions of that medium?
- How did the author intend the image to be viewed originally?
- How has the image been reproduced, what meaning is thus lent to it?

Questions to Help You Analyze Images

Here are some specific questions for you to consider as you begin writing about visual images. You might keep in mind that your response to a visual image may depend on whether it is print-based or electronic. To start with, you could think about the general mood of the image. What sort of response does the image attempt to evoke? How is the image designed? How are the visual elements of the image arranged in relation to each other, and how do they occupy and are framed within the space? Look at what is in the foreground and the background. What might this tell you about the message being communicated? Once again, consider the Iwo Jima photograph to illustrate a point. Does the image include textual elements and at what point in its (re)production? While words were not originally included in the war photograph, when it appeared in newspapers or in newsreels, it undoubtedly would have had a caption or title. What does the appearance of language contribute to the meaning of image? What is the immediate context of the image; that is, what issues currently in society does the image draw upon? How is the photograph displayed and what does that tell you about the values it represents? Also, is there a broader context you might identify? Does the image make reference in some way to some larger issue? In this manner, how do images in general, or any visual material, make their arguments? How to they attempt to create belief and persuade you of something by what they include and what they leave out? Visual material has its own way of working on the viewer. Even things as seemingly simple as graphs and charts compress and organize their information in certain ways to convey a point of view. Analyzing images can be an entertaining way to sharpen one's critical skills. Also, the ability to interpret images can be very useful, given that we live in a world so dominated by images. To think of images as texts gives us a framework for interpreting their meaning and their effect on our lives.

Henry Martin

This 1987 cartoon published in The New Yorker, *plays with the meaning of the word* block, *which can indicate either a child's toy or a disabling form of anxiety that keeps writers from writing. The spelling rules and the punctuation marks depicted on the faces of the block are probably not the causes of any real incidents of writer's block. However, they are just the sorts of excuses that some inexperienced writers use to justify their tendency to avoid the hard work of writing.*

Questions on Meaning

1. Do spelling and punctuation rules make you anxious when you're writing? If so, explain how you deal with the anxiety.
2. Explain the pun in this cartoon. How does the information on the "block" relate to writer's block, a condition in which anxiety prevents a writer from working?

Questions on Rhetorical Strategy and Style

1. This cartoon can be read as a theory about how writer's block arises in young writers. Explain the specific theory that the cartoonist might be advancing.
2. The cartoon might also be read as an ironic comment on writing anxiety; that is, an invitation to writers to get over it. Explain how the cartoon could be used to support that point.

Writing Assignments

1. Research on the writing process suggests that anxiety often stems from a writer's rigidity about "rules." Write an essay that describes your own writing process, focusing on the customs and rules that shape your work. Note rules that make it difficult for you to complete your work.
2. Write an essay describing one or more pieces of writing that gave you trouble. Try to represent the problem of writing in a more complex and realistic way than the oversimplification presented in this cartoon.

☙ WRITING ☜

William Stafford

William Stafford (1914–1993) grew up in Kansas and taught at Lewis and Clark College in Oregon. His books include Traveling Through the Dark *(1963), which received the National Book Award;* Stories That Could Be True *(1977), a collection of poems;* Writing the Australian Crawl *(1978), a collection of essays;* A Glass Face in the Rain *(1982);* You Must Revise Your Life *(1986), another collection of essays;* An Oregon Message *(1987); and* Passwords *(1991). Stafford describes a writing process that works for him—and might for you—in this timeless 1970 essay.*

1   A writer is not so much someone who has something to say as he is someone who has found a process that will bring about new things he would not have thought of if he had not started to say them. That is, he does not draw on a reservoir; instead, he engages in an activity that brings to him a whole succession of unforeseen stories, poems, essays, plays, laws, philosophies, religions, or—but wait!

Back in school, from the first when I began to try to write things, I felt this richness. One thing would lead to another; the world would give and give. Now, after twenty years or so of trying, I live by that certain richness, an idea hard to pin, difficult to say, and perhaps offensive to some. For there are strange implications in it.

One implication is the importance of just plain receptivity. When I write, I like to have an interval before me when I am not likely to be interrupted. For me, this means usually the early morning, before others are awake. I get pen and paper, take a glance out the window (often it is dark out there), and wait. It is like fishing. But I do not wait very long, for there is always a nibble—and this is where receptivity comes

Excerpted from "A Way of Writing.", *Field: Contemporary Poetry and Poetics,* no. 2. Published by Oberlin College Press.

in. To get started I will accept anything that occurs to me. Something always occurs, of course, to any of us. We can't keep from thinking. Maybe I have to settle for an immediate impression: it's cold, or hot, or dark, or bright, or in between! Or—well, the possibilities are endless. If I put down something, that thing will help the next thing come, and I'm off. If I let the process go on, things will occur to me that were not at all in my mind when I started. These things, odd and trivial as they may be, are somehow connected. And if I let them string out, surprising things will happen.

If I let them string out . . . Along with initial receptivity, then, there is another readiness: I must be willing to fail. If I am to keep on writing, I cannot bother to insist on high standards. I must get into action and not let anything stop me, or even slow me much. By "standards" I do not mean "correctness"—spelling, punctuation, and so on. These details become mechanical for anyone who writes for a while. I am thinking about what many people would consider "important" standards, such matters as social significance, positive values, consistency, etc. I resolutely disregard these. Something better, greater, is happening! I am following a process that leads so wildly and originally into new territory that no judgment can at the moment be made about values, significance, and so on. I am making something new, something that has not been judged before. Later others—and maybe I myself—will make judgments. Now, I am headlong to discover. Any distraction may harm the creating.

So, receptive, careless of failure, I spin out things on the page. And a wonderful freedom comes. If something occurs to me, it is all right to accept it. It has one justification: it occurs to me. No one else can guide me. I must follow my own weak, wandering, diffident impulses.

A strange bonus happens. At times, without my insisting on it, my writings become coherent; the successive elements that occur to me are clearly related. They lead by themselves to new connections. Sometimes the language, even the syllables that happen along, may start a trend. Sometimes the materials alert me to something waiting in my mind, ready for sustained attention. At such times, I allow myself to be eloquent, or intentional, or for great swoops (treacherous! not to be trusted!) reasonable. But I do not insist on any of that; for I know that back of my activity there will be the coherence of my self, and that indulgence of my impulses will bring recurrent patterns and meanings again.

This attitude toward the process of writing creatively suggests a problem for me, in terms of what others say. They talk about "skills" in writing. Without denying that I do have experience, wide reading, automatic orthodoxies and maneuvers of various kinds, I still must insist that I am often baffled about what "skill" has to do with the precious little area of confusion when I do not know what I am going to say and then I found out what I am going to say. That precious interval I am unable to bridge by skill. What can I witness about it? It remains mysterious, just as all of us must feel puzzled about how we are so inventive as to be able to talk along through complexities with our friends, not needing to plan what we are going to say, but never stalled for long in our confident forward progress. Skill? If so, it is the skill we all have, something we must have learned before the age of three or four.

A writer is one who has become accustomed to trusting that grace, or luck, or—skill.

Yet another attitude I find necessary: most of what I write, like most of what I say in casual conversation, will not amount to much. Even I will realize, and even at the time, that it is not negotiable. It will be like practice. In conversation, I allow myself random remarks—in fact, as I recall, that is the way I learned to talk—so in writing I launch many expendable efforts. A result of this free way of writing is that I am not writing for others, mostly; they will not see the product at all unless the activity eventuates in something that later appears to be worthy. My guide is the self, and its adventuring in the language brings about communication.

This process-rather-than-substance view of writing invites a final, dual reflection:

1. Writers may not be special—sensitive or talented in any usual sense. They are simply engaged in sustained use of a language skill we all have. Their "creations" come about through confident reliance on stray impulses that will, with trust, find occasional patterns that are satisfying.

2. But writing itself is one of the great, free human activities. There is scope for individuality, and elation, and discovery, in writing. For the person who follows with trust and forgiveness what occurs to him, the world remains always ready and deep, an inexhaustible environment, with the combined vividness of an actuality and flexibility of a dream. Working back and forth between experience and thought, writers have more than space and time can offer. They have the whole unexplored realm of human vision.

Questions on Meaning

1. Compare and contrast Stafford's thesis as it applies to fiction versus nonfiction (such as reports).
2. What does Stafford mean by not insisting on high standards? Why does he insist that writers be "willing to fail"?
3. Stafford states that writers "may not be special," but they are different. In what way do writers use "a language skill we all have"?

Questions on Rhetorical Strategy and Style

1. Find where Stafford defines what a writer is (or isn't). Compare his definition of a writer to your perception of what characterizes a writer. Describe what bests defines *you* as a writer.
2. Reread the essay and show how Stafford analyzes his writing process. Compare and contrast his rhetorical strategy of narration to a how-to list of steps. Explain which writing technique you prefer for this material.

Writing Assignments

1. Practice what Stafford preaches: At a time when you will not be disturbed, sit down and write. Afterward, assess your experience. Were you inhibited by the "substance"? Did you feel the "freedom" expressed by Stafford? Explain why his technique would or would not work for you.
2. To Stafford, "just plain receptivity" is important to successful writing. What other pursuits depend on opening your mind the way Stafford describes? Write an essay about an experience you have had—perhaps in painting, composing, or dance—in which your "receptivity" contributed to your creativity. Describe the process you used to engaged your "receptivity." What was the result? How did the experience affect subsequent creative sessions?

❧ MOTHER TONGUE ❧

Amy Tan

Amy Tan was born in Oakland, California in 1952, several years after her mother and father immigrated from China. She was raised in various cities in the San Francisco Bay Area. When she was eight, her essay, "What the Library Means to Me," won first prize among elementary school participants, for which Tan received a transistor radio and publication in the local newspaper. Upon the deaths of her brother and father in 1967 and 1968 from brain tumors, the family began a haphazard journey through Europe, before settling in Montreux, Switzerland, where Tan graduated in her junior year in 1969.

For the next seven years, Tan attended five schools. She first went to Linfield College in McMinnville, Oregon, and there, on a blind date, met her future husband, Lou DeMattei. She followed him to San Jose, where she enrolled in San Jose City College. She next attended San Jose State University, and, while working two part-time jobs, she became an English honor's students and a President's Scholar, while carrying a semester course load of 21 units. In 1972 she graduated with honors, receiving a B.A. with a double major in English and Linguistics. She was awarded a scholarship to attend the Summer Linguistics Institute at the University of California, Santa Cruz. In 1973, she earned her M.A. in Linguistics, also from San Jose State University, and was then awarded a Graduate Minority Fellowship under the affirmative action program at the University of California, Berkeley, where she enrolled as a doctoral student in linguistics.

First published in *Threepenny Review,* 1990. Copyright © 1990 by Amy Tan.

I am not a scholar of English or literature. I cannot give you much more than personal opinions on the English language and its variations in this country or others.

I am a writer. And by that definition, I am someone who has always loved language. I am fascinated by language in daily life. I spend a great deal of my time thinking about the power of language—the way it can evoke an emotion, a visual image, a complex idea, or a simple truth. Language is the tool of my trade. And I use them all—all the Englishes I grew up with.

Recently, I was made keenly aware of the different Englishes I do use. I was giving a talk to a large group of people, the same talk I had already given to half a dozen other groups. The nature of the talk was about my writing, my life, and my book, *The Joy Luck Club*. The talk was going along well enough, until I remembered one major difference that made the whole talk sound wrong. My mother was in the room. And it was perhaps the first time she had heard me give a lengthy speech, using the kind of English I have never used with her. I was saying things like, "The intersection of memory upon imagination" and "There is an aspect of my fiction that relates to thus-and-thus"—a speech filled with carefully wrought grammatical phrases, burdened, it suddenly seemed to me, with nominalized forms, past perfect tenses, conditional phrases, all the forms of standard English that I had learned in school and through books, the forms of English I did not use at home with my mother.

Just last week, I was walking down the street with my mother, and I again found myself conscious of the English I was using, and the English I do use with her. We were talking about the price of new and used furniture and I heard myself saying this: "Not waste money that way." My husband was with us as well, and he didn't notice any switch in my English. And then I realized why. It's because over the twenty years we've been together I've often used that same kind of English with him, and sometimes he even uses it with me. It has become our language of intimacy, a different sort of English that relates to family talk, the language I grew up with.

So you'll have some idea of what this family talk I heard sounds like, I'll quote what my mother said during a recent conversation which I videotaped and then transcribed. During this conversation, my mother was talking about a political gangster in Shanghai who had the same last name as her family's, Du, and how the gangster in his early years wanted to be adopted by her family, which was rich by comparison. Later, the gangster became more powerful, far richer than my mother's family, and one day showed up at my mother's wedding to pay his respects. Here's what she said in part:

"Du Yusong having business like fruit stand. Like off the street kind. He is Du like Du Zong—but not Tsung-ming Island people. The local people call putong, the river east side, he belong to that side local people. That man want to ask Du Zong father take him in like become own family. Du Zong father wasn't look down on him, but didn't take seriously, until that man big like become a mafia. Now important person, very hard to inviting him. Chinese way, came only to show respect, don't stay for dinner. Respect for making big celebration, he shows up. Mean gives lots of respect. Chinese custom. Chinese social life that way. If too important won't have to stay too long. He come to my wedding. I didn't see, I heard it. I gone to boy's side, they have YMCA dinner. Chinese age I was nineteen."

You should know that my mother's expressive command of English belies how much she actually understands. She reads the *Forbes* report, listens to *Wall Street Week*, converses daily with her stockbroker, reads all of Shirley MacLaine's books with ease—all kinds of things I can't begin to understand. Yet some of my friends tell me they understand 50 percent of what my mother says. Some say they understand 80 to 90 percent. Some say they understand none of it, as if she were speaking pure Chinese. But to me, my mother's English is perfectly clear, perfectly natural. It's my mother tongue. Her language, as I hear it, is vivid, direct, full of observation and imagery. That was the language that helped shape the way I saw things, expressed things, made sense of the world.

Lately, I've been giving more thought to the kind of English my mother speaks. Like others, I have described it to people as "broken" or "fractured" English. But I wince when I say that. It has always bothered me that I can think of no way to describe it other than "broken," as if it were damaged and needed to be fixed, as if it lacked a certain wholeness and soundness. I've heard other terms used, "limited English," for example. But they seem just as bad, as if everything is limited, including people's perceptions of the limited English speaker.

I know this for a fact, because when I was growing up, my mother's "limited" English limited *my* perception of her. I was ashamed of her English. I believed that her English reflected the quality of what she had to say. That is, because she expressed them imperfectly her thoughts were imperfect. And I had plenty of empirical evidence to support me: the fact that people in department stores, at banks, and at restaurants did not take her seriously, did not give her good service, pretended not to understand her, or even acted as if they did not hear her.

10   My mother has long realized the limitations of her English as well.   10
When I was fifteen, she used to have me call people on the phone to pretend I was she. In this guise, I was forced to ask for information or even to complain and yell at people who had been rude to her. One time it was a call to her stockbroker in New York. She had cashed out her small portfolio and it just so happened we were going to go to New York the next week, our very first trip outside California. I had to get on the phone and say in an adolescent voice that was not very convincing, "This is Mrs. Tan."

And my mother was standing in the back whispering loudly, "Why he don't send me check, already two weeks late. So mad he lie to me, losing me money."

And then I said in perfect English, "Yes, I'm getting rather concerned. You had agreed to send the check two weeks ago, but it hasn't arrived."

Then she began to talk more loudly. "What he want, I come to New York tell him front of his boss, you cheating me?" And I was trying to calm her down, make her be quiet, while telling the stockbroker, "I can't tolerate any more excuses. If I don't receive the check immediately, I am going to have to speak to your manager when I'm in New York next week." And sure enough, the following week there we were in front of this astonished stockbroker, and I was sitting there red-faced and quiet, and my mother, the real Mrs. Tan, was shouting at his boss in her impeccable broken English.

We used a similar routine just five days ago, for a situation that was far less humorous. My mother had gone to the hospital for an appointment, to find out about a benign brain tumor a CAT scan had revealed a month ago. She said she had spoken very good English, her best English, no mistakes. Still, she said, the hospital did not apologize when they said they had lost the CAT scan and she had come for nothing. She said they did not seem to have any sympathy when she told them she was anxious to know the exact diagnosis, since her husband and son had both died of brain tumors. She said they would not give her any more information until the next time and she would have to make another appointment for that. So she said she would not leave until the doctor called her daughter. She wouldn't budge. And when the doctor finally called her daughter, me, who spoke in perfect English—lo and behold—we had assurances the CAT scan would be found, promises that a conference call on Monday would be held, and apologies for any suffering my mother had gone through for a most regrettable mistake.

15   I think my mother's English almost had an effect on limiting my possibilities in life as well. Sociologists and linguists probably will tell you that a person's developing language skills are more influenced by peers. But I do think that the language spoken in the family, especially in immigrant families which are more insular, plays a large role in shaping the language of the child. And I believe that it affected my results on achievement tests, IQ tests, and the SAT. While my English skills were never judged as poor, compared to math, English could not be considered my strong suit. In grade school I did moderately well, getting perhaps B's, sometimes B-pluses, in English and scoring perhaps in the sixtieth or seventieth percentile on achievement tests. But those scores were not good enough to override the opinion that my true abilities lay in math and science, because in those areas I achieved A's and scored in the ninetieth percentile or higher.

This was understandable. Math is precise, there is only one correct answer. Whereas, for me at least, the answers on English tests were always a judgment call, a matter of opinion and personal experience. Those tests were constructed around items like fill-in-the-blank sentence completion, Such as, "Even though Tom was _____, Mary thought he was _____." And the correct answer always seemed to be the most bland combinations of thoughts, for example, "Even though Tom was shy, Mary thought he was charming," with the grammatical structure "even though" limiting the correct answer to some sort of semantic opposites, so you wouldn't get answers like, Even though Tom was foolish, Mary thought he was ridiculous." Well, according to my mother, there were very few limitations as to what Tom could have been and what Mary might have thought of him. So I never did well on tests like that.

The same was true with word analogies, pairs of words in which you were supposed to find some sort of logical, semantic relationship—

for example, "*Sunset* is to *nightfall* as _____ is to _____."
And here you would be presented with a list of four possible pairs, one
of which showed the same kind of relationship: *red* is to *stoplight, bus*
is to *arrival, chills* is to *fever, yawn* is to *boring*. Well, I could never think
that way. I knew what the tests were asking, but I could not block out
of my mind the images already created by the first pair, "*sunset* is to
nightfall"—and I would see a burst of colors against a darkening sky,
the moon rising, the lowering of a curtain of stars. And all the other
pairs of words—red, bus, stoplight, boring—just threw up a mass of
confusing images, making it impossible for me to sort out something
as logical as saying: "A sunset precedes nightfall" is the same as "a chill
precedes a fever." The only way I would have gotten that answer right
would have been to imagine an associative situation, for example, my
being disobedient and staying out past sunset, catching a chill at night,
which turns into feverish pneumonia as punishment, which indeed did
happen to me.

I have been thinking about all this lately, about my mother's English,
about achievement tests. Because lately I've been asked, as a writer,
why there are not more Asian Americans represented in American literature. Why are there few Asian Americans enrolled in creative writing programs? Why do so many Chinese students go into engineering?
Well, these are broad sociological questions I can't begin to answer.
But I have noticed in surveys—in fact, just last week—that Asian students, as a whole, always do significantly better on math achievement
tests than in English. And this makes me think that there are other
Asian American students whose English spoken in the home might
also be described as "broken" or "limited." And perhaps they also have
teachers who are steering them away from writing and into math and
science, which is what happened to me.

Fortunately, I happen to be rebellious in nature and enjoy the
challenge of disproving assumptions made about me. I became an
English major my first year in college, after being enrolled as pre-med.
I started writing nonfiction as a freelancer the week after I was told by
my former boss that writing was my worst skill and I should hone my
talents toward account management.

20   But it wasn't until 1985 that I finally began to write fiction. And   20
at first I wrote using what I thought to be wittily crafted sentences,
sentences that would finally prove I had mastery over the English

language. Here's an example from the first draft of a story that later made its way into *The Joy Luck Club,* but without this line: "That was my mental quandary in its nascent state." A terrible line, which I can barely pronounce.

Fortunately, for reasons I won't get into today, I later decided I should envision a reader for the stories I would write. And the reader I decided upon was my mother, because these were stories about mothers. So with this reader in mind—and in fact she did read my early drafts—I began to write stories using all the Englishes I grew up with: the English I spoke to my mother, which for lack of a better term might be described as "simple"; the English she used with me, which for lack of a better term might be described as "broken"; my translation of her Chinese, which could certainly be described as "watered down"; and what I imagined to be her translation of her Chinese if she could speak in perfect English, her internal language, and for that I sought to preserve the essence, but neither an English nor a Chinese structure. I wanted to capture what language ability tests can never reveal: her intent, her passion, her imagery, the rhythms of her speech and the nature of her thoughts.

Apart from what any critic had to say about my writing, I knew I had succeeded where it counted when my mother finished reading my book and gave me her verdict: "So easy to read."

Questions on Meaning

1. Until near the end of the essay, Tan describes essentially only two "Englishes": the English with which she speaks to others, as in the speech she delivers, and the English of her mother. At the end we learn of a multitude of other Englishes. What are these? What are the differences among them?
2. Why was Tan ashamed of her mother's English when she was growing up?
3. What does Tan have to say about her math scores being higher than her language scores?

Questions on Rhetorical Strategy and Style

4. Tan uses the writing strategy of narration to reveal how others reacted to her mother's language skills, such as the treatment she received at the hospital. Reread that scene and explain how it effectively develops Tan's point.
5. Tan says that she wanted in her writing to capture her mother's "intent, her passion, her imagery, the rhythms of her speech and the nature of her thoughts." Evaluate this essay by this standard: do we get a glimpse of her mother's character here? How does Tan use language in this essay to capture a small part of her mother?

Writing Assignments

1. Tan makes the point that teachers may be steering Asian American students into math and science because their language scores may mistakenly be suggesting they have lower aptitude in studies involving language. Could such "steering" by teachers and guidance counselors be faulty with other students as well? Think of some other examples of situations in which test scores could give false impressions about a person's natural abilities and aptitudes.
2. Tan describes how people judged her mother as a result of her "broken English." What other ways do people judge strangers by appearances? Do clothing and physical appearance give true insight into what a person is like? Write an essay in which you explore the issue of how we come to know what people are like and the extent to which it is meaningful to make assumptions based on how people look and sound.

3. Tan explains at length how she never understood word analogy tests because her mind just did not work that way. Is this more than just a matter of using English? Are there differences in how people think that can throw off such responses to standardized tests, such as those used to measure intelligence? Write an essay in which you explain your ideas, based on your own experience, about whether standardized tests accurately measure people's abilities and aptitudes.

❧ THAT WORD *BLACK* ❧

Langston Hughes

Langston Hughes (1902–1967), a poet, short-story writer, essayist, and playwright, was born in Joplin, Missouri, and grew up in Kansas and Ohio. After graduating from high school (where he began writing poetry), Hughes spent 15 months in Mexico with his father, attended Columbia University for a year, worked as a seaman on cargo ships bound to Africa and Europe, and bused tables at a hotel in New York City. Later, he returned to school and graduated from Lincoln University (1929). Part of the "Harlem Renaissance" or "New Negro Renaissance"—and fiercely proud of his African-American heritage—Hughes often drew from Negro spirituals and blues and jazz in his literary work. Hughes was published in Amsterdam News, Crisis, The New Negro, *and other periodicals. His books include the novel* Not Without Laughter *(1930); the short story collection* The Ways of White Folks *(1934); the play* The Mulatto *(1935); his autobiography* The Big Sea *(1940); and his poetry collections* The Weary Blues *(1926),* Shakespeare of Harlem *(1942),* Montage of a Dream Deferred *(1951), and* Ask Your Mama *(1961). In this essay, through his character "Simple," Hughes shows how the word "black" has acquired many negative connotations.*

1   "This evening," said Simple, "I feel like talking about the word black."

"Nobody's stopping you, so go ahead. But what you really ought to have is a soap-box out on the corner of 126th and Lenox where the rest of the orators hang out."

"They expresses some good ideas on that corner," said Simple, "but for my ideas I do not need a crowd. Now, as I were saying, the word *black*, white folks have done used that word to mean something bad so often until now when the N.A.A.C.P asks for civil rights for the black man, they think they must be bad. Looking back into history, I reckon it all started with a *black* cat meaning bad luck. Don't let one cross your path!

"Next, somebody got up a *blacklist* on which you get if you don't vote right. Then when lodges come into being, the folks they didn't want in them got *blackballed.* If you kept a skeleton in your closet, you might get *blackmailed.* And everything bad was *black.* When it came down to the unlucky ball on the pool table, the eight-rock, they made it the *black* ball. So no wonder there ain't no equal rights for the *black* man."

"All you say is true about the odium attached to the word *black,*" I said. "You've even forgotten a few. For example, during the war if you bought something under the table, illegally, they said you were trading on the *black* market. In Chicago, if you're a gangster, the *Black Hand Society* may take you for a ride. And certainly if you don't behave yourself, your family will say you're a *black* sheep. Then, if your mama burns a *black* candle to change the family luck, they call it *black* magic."

"My mama never did believe in voodoo so she did not burn no black candles," said Simple.

"If she had, that would have been a *black* mark against her."

"Stop talking about my mama. What I want to know is, where do white folks get off calling everything bad *black*? If it is a dark night, they say it's *black* as hell. If you are mean and evil, they say you got a *black* heart. I would like to change all that around and say that the people who Jim Crow me have got a *white* heart. People who sell dope to children have got a *white* mark against them. And all the white gamblers who were behind the basketball fix are the *white* sheep of the sports world. God knows there was few, if any, Negroes selling stuff on the black market during the war, so why didn't they call it the *white* market? No, they got to take me and my color and turn it into everything bad. According to white folks, black is bad.

"Wait till my day comes! In my language, bad will be *white.* Blackmail will be *white*mail. Black cats will be good luck, and *white* cats will be bad. If a *white* cat crosses your path, look out! I will take the black ball for the cue ball and let the *white* ball be the unlucky eight-rock. And on my blacklist—which will be a *white*list then—I will put everybody who ever Jim Crowed me from Rankin to Hitler, Talmadge to Malan, South Carolina to South Africa.

10   "I am black. When I look in the mirror, I see myself, daddy-o, but   10
I am not ashamed. God made me. He also made F.D., dark as he is.
He did not make us no badder than the rest of the folks. The earth is
black and all kinds of good things comes out of the earth. Trees and
flowers and fruit and sweet potatoes and corn and all that keeps mens
alive comes right up out of the earth—good old black earth. Coal is
black and it warms your house and cooks your food. The night is
black, which has a moon, and a million stars, and is beautiful. Sleep
is black which gives you rest, so you wake up feeling good. I am black.
I feel very good this evening.

         "What is wrong with black?"

Questions on Meaning

1. Why does Simple declare that "civil rights" mean something "bad" to white people?
2. How does Simple intend to reverse the negative connotations attached to the word *black*?
3. What is Hughes' thesis in this piece? Is it explicitly stated?

Questions on Rhetorical Strategy and Style

1. Hughes wrote this piece entirely in dialogue. Describe the effect on his delivery—and message—if he had used a narrative form, without dialogue. How does the interaction between the speakers help strengthen his arguments?
2. What examples does Hughes give of negative word forms incorporating *black*? What positive uses of *black* does he give?
3. In addition to *two* speakers and *two* colors, how else does Hughes use duality in this essay?
4. Choose five of the negative word forms using *black* and use each in a sentence. Next, rewrite the sentence, replacing the offensive word form with another expression. How difficult is it to eliminate these words? Explain how the revised sentences differ in meaning from the original sentence.

Writing Assignments

1. Write an essay on the use of politically correct speech—such as using "chairperson" rather than "chairman" or using contractions, such as "s/he." Explain why you feel these more sensitive word choices are necessary or not. Provide recommendations for acceptable writing today.
2. Look up the word *black* in the Oxford English Dictionary. Report the changes in meaning the word has undergone since its first recorded use in English.

HATE RADIO

Patricia J. Williams

*Patricia Williams (1951–) was born in Boston, Massa-
chusetts and educated amongst the privileged students of
Wellesley and Harvard Law School. She has written articles for newspapers such as the* Boston Globe, *the* Christian Science Monitor, *and the* Washington Post; *as well
as for magazines such as* Ms., The Nation, *and the* New
Yorker. *She has written two books on race issues:* The
Alchemy of Race and Rights *(1991) and* The Rooster's
Egg: On the Persistence of Prejudice *(1995). She has
taught at Golden Gate University, the City University of
New York, the University of Wisconsin, and presently
teaches at Columbia University. In this essay first published
in* Ms. *in 1994, Williams describes an unattractive aspect
of the post-modern environment, the rise of radio programming that uses extremist views involving racism and
sexism as "entertainment."*

1   Three years ago I stood at my sink, washing the dishes and listening to the radio. I was tuned to rock and roll so I could
avoid thinking about the big news from the day before—
George Bush had just nominated Clarence Thomas to replace Thurgood Marshall on the Supreme Court. I was squeezing a dot of lemon
Joy into each of the wineglasses when I realized that two smoothly
radio-cultured voices, a man's and a woman's, had replaced the music.

"I think it's a stroke of genius on the president's part," said the female voice.

"Yeah," said the male voice. "Then those blacks, those African
Americans, those Negroes—hey 'Negro' is good enough for Thurgood
Marshall—whatever, they can't make up their minds [what] they want
to be called. I'm gonna call them Blafricans. Black Africans. Yeah, I

---

like it. Blafricans. Then they can get all upset because now the president appointed a Blafrican."

'Yeah, well, that's the way those liberals think. It's just crazy."

5 "And then after they turn down his nomination the president can say he tried to please 'em, and then he can appoint someone with some intelligence."

Back then, this conversation seemed so horrendously unusual, so singularly hateful, that I picked up a pencil and wrote it down. I was certain that a firestorm of protest was going to engulf the station and purge those foul radio mouths with the good clean soap of social outrage.

I am so naive. When I finally turned on the radio and rolled my dial to where everyone else had been tuned while I was busy watching Cosby reruns, it took me a while to understand that there's a firestorm all right, but not of protest. In the two and a half years since Thomas has assumed his post on the Supreme Court, the underlying assumptions of the conversation I heard as uniquely outrageous have become commonplace, popularly expressed, and louder in volume. I hear the style of that snide polemicism everywhere, among acquaintances, on the street, on television in toned-down versions. It is a crude demagoguery that makes me heartsick. I feel more and more surrounded by that point of view, the assumptions of being without intelligence, the coded epithets, the "Blafrican"-like stand-ins for "nigger," the mocking angry glee, the endless tirades filled with nonspecific, nonempirically based slurs against "these people" or "those minorities" or "feminazis" or "liberals" or "scumbags" or "pansies" or "jerks" or "sleazeballs" or "loonies" or "animals" or "foreigners."

At the same time I am not so naive as to suppose that this is something new. In clearheaded moments I realize I am not listening to the radio anymore, I am listening to a large segment of white America think aloud in ever louder resurgent thoughts that have generations of historical precedent. It's as though the radio has split open like an egg, Morton Downey, Jr.'s clones and Joe McCarthy's ghost spilling out, broken yolks, a great collective of sometimes clever, sometimes small, but uniformly threatened brains—they have all come gushing out. Just as they were about to pass into oblivion, Jack Benny and his humble black sidekick Rochester get resurrected in the ungainly bodies of Howard Stern and his faithful black henchwoman, Robin Quivers. The culture of Amos and Andy has been revived and reassembled in

Bob Grant's radio minstrelry and radio newcomer Daryl Gates's sanctimonious imprecations on behalf of decent white people. And in striking imitation of Jesse Helms's nearly forgotten days as a radio host, the far Right has found its undisputed king in the personage of Rush Limbaugh—a polished demagogue with a weekly radio audience of at least twenty million, a television show that vies for ratings with the likes of Jay Leno, a newsletter with a circulation of 380,000, and two best-selling books whose combined sales are closing in on six million copies.

From Churchill to Hitler to the old Soviet Union, it's clear that radio and television have the power to change the course of history, to proselytize, and to coalesce not merely the good and the noble, but the very worst in human nature as well. Likewise, when Orson Welles made his famous radio broadcast "witnessing" the landing of a spaceship full of hostile Martians, the United States ought to have learned a lesson about the power of radio to appeal to mass instincts and incite mass hysteria. Radio remains a peculiarly powerful medium even today, its visual emptiness in a world of six trillion flashing images allowing one of the few remaining playgrounds for the aural subconscious. Perhaps its power is attributable to our need for an oral tradition after all, some conveying of stories, feelings, myths of ancestors, epics of alienation, and the need to rejoin ancestral roots, even ignorant bigoted roots. Perhaps the visual quiescence of radio is related to the popularity of E-mail or electronic networking. Only the voice is made manifest, unmasking worlds that cannot—or dare not?—be seen. Just yet. Nostalgia crystallizing into a dangerous future. The preconscious voice erupting into the expressed, the prime time.

10   What comes out of the modern radio mouth could be the *Iliad*,   10
the *Rubáiyát*, the griot's song of our times. If indeed radio is a vessel for the American "Song of Songs," then what does it mean that a manic, adolescent Howard Stern is so popular among radio listeners, that Rush Limbaugh's wittily smooth sadism has gone the way of prime-time television, and that both vie for the number one slot on all the best-selling book lists? What to make of the stories being told by our modern radio evangelists and their tragic unloved chorus of callers? Is it really just a collapsing economy that spawns this drama of grown people sitting around scaring themselves to death with fantasies of black feminist Mexican able-bodied gay soldiers earning $100,000

a year on welfare who are so criminally depraved that Hillary Clinton or the Antichrist-of-the-moment had no choice but to invite them onto the government payroll so they can run the country? The panicky exaggeration reminds me of a child's fear. . . . *And then, and then, a huge lion jumped out of the shadows and was about to gobble me up, and I can't ever sleep again for a whole week.*

As I spin the dial on my radio, I can't help thinking that this stuff must be related to that most poignant of fiber-optic phenomena, phone sex. Aural Sex, Radio Racism and a touch of S & M. High-priest hosts with the power and run-amok ego to discipline listeners, to smack with the verbal back of the hand, to smash the button that shuts you up once and for all. "Idiot!" shouts New York City radio demagogue Bob Grant and then the sound of droning telephone emptiness, the voice of dissent dumped out some trapdoor in aural space.

As I listened to a range of such programs what struck me as the most unifying theme was not merely the specific intolerance on such hot topics as race and gender, but a much more general contempt for the world, a verbal stoning of anything different. It is like some unusually violent game of "Simon Says," this mockery and shouting down of callers, this roar of incantations, the insistence on agreement.

But, ah, if you *will* but only agree, what sweet and safe reward, what soft enfolding by a stern and angry radio god. And as an added bonus, the invisible shield of an AM community, a family of fans who are Exactly Like You, to whom you can express, in anonymity, all the filthy stuff you imagine "them" doing to you. The comfort and relief of being able to ejaculate, to those who understand, about the dark imagined excess overtaking, robbing, needing to be held down and taught a good lesson, needing to put it in its place before the ravenous demon enervates all that is true and good and pure in this life.

The audience for this genre of radio flagellation is mostly young, white, and male. Two thirds of Rush Limbaugh's audience is male. According to *Time* magazine, 75 percent of Howard Stern's listeners are white men. Most of the callers have spent their lives walling themselves off from any real experience with blacks, feminists, lesbians, or gays. In this regard, it is probably true, as former Secretary of Education William Bennett says, that Rush Limbaugh "tells his audience that what you believe inside, you can talk about in the marketplace." Unfortunately, what's "inside" is then mistaken for what's outside, treated as empirical and political reality. The *National Review* extols

Limbaugh's conservative leadership as no less than that of Ronald Reagan, and the Republican party provides Limbaugh with books to discuss, stories, angles, and public support. "People were afraid of censure by gay activists, feminists, environmentalists—now they are not because Rush takes them on," says Bennett.

15   U.S. history has been marked by cycles in which brands of this or   15
that hatred come into fashion and go out, are unleashed and then restrained. If racism, homophobia, jingoism, and woman-hating have been features of national life in pretty much all of modern history, it rather begs the question to spend a lot of time wondering if right-wing radio is a symptom or a cause. For at least 400 years, prevailing attitudes in the West have considered African Americans less intelligent. Recent statistics show that 53 percent of people in the United States agree that blacks and Latinos are less intelligent than whites, and a majority believe that blacks are lazy, violent, welfare-dependent, and unpatriotic.

I think that what has made life more or less tolerable for "out" groups have been those moments in history when those "inside" feelings were relatively restrained. In fact, if I could believe that right-wing radio were only about idiosyncratic, singular, rough-hewn individuals thinking those inside thoughts, I'd be much more inclined to agree with Columbia University media expert Everette Dennis, who says that Stern's and Limbaugh's popularity represents the "triumph of the individual" or with *Time* magazine's bottom line that "the fact that either is seriously considered a threat . . . is more worrisome than Stern or Limbaugh will ever be." If what I were hearing had even a tad more to do with real oppressions, with real white *and* black levels of joblessness and homelessness, or with the real problems of real white men, then I wouldn't have bothered to slog my way through hours of Howard Stern's miserable obsessions.

Yet at the heart of my anxiety is the worry that Stern, Limbaugh, Grant, et al. represent the very antithesis of individualism's triumph. As the *National Review* said of Limbaugh's ascent, "It was a feat not only of the loudest voice but also of a keen political brain to round up, as Rush did, the media herd and drive them into the conservative corral." When asked about his political aspirations, Bob Grant gloated to the *Washington Post,* "I think I would make rather a good dictator."

The polemics of right-wing radio are putting nothing less than hate onto the airwaves, into the marketplace, electing it to office, teaching it in schools, and exalting it as freedom. What worries me is the increasing-to-constant commerce of retribution, control, and lashing out, fed not by fact but fantasy. What worries me is the reemergence, more powerfully than at any time since the institution of Jim Crow, of a socio-centered self that excludes "the likes of," well, me for example, from the civic circle, and that would rob me of my worth and claim and identity as a citizen. As the *Economist* rightly observes, "Mr. Limbaugh takes a mass market—white, mainly male, middle-class, ordinary America—and talks to it as an endangered minority."

I worry about this identity whose external reference is a set of beliefs, ethics, and practices that excludes, restricts, and acts in the world on me, or mine, as the perceived if not real enemy. I am acutely aware of losing *my* mythic individualism to the surface shapes of my mythic group fearsomeness as black, as female, as left wing. "I" merge not fluidly but irretrievably into a category of "them." I become a suspect self, a moving target of loathsome properties, not merely different but dangerous. And that worries me a lot.

20   What happens in my life with all this translated license, this permission to be uncivil? What happens to the social space that was supposedly at the sweet mountaintop of the civil rights movement's trail? Can I get a seat on the bus without having to be reminded that I *should* be standing? Did the civil rights movement guarantee us nothing more than to use public accommodations while surrounded by raving lunatic bigots? "They didn't beat this idiot [Rodney King] enough," says Howard Stern.

Not long ago I had the misfortune to hail a taxicab in which the driver was listening to Howard Stern undress some woman. After some blocks, I had to get out. I was, frankly, afraid to ask the driver to turn it off—not because I was afraid of "censoring" him, which seems to be the only thing people will talk about anymore, but because the driver was stripping me too, as he leered through the rearview mirror. "Something the matter?" he demanded, as I asked him to pull over and let me out well short of my destination. (I'll spare you the full story of what happened from there—trying to get another cab, as the cabbies stopped for all the white businessmen who so much as scratched their heads near the curb; a nice young white man, seeing my plight, giving me his cab, having to thank him, he hero, me saved-but-humiliated, cabdriver pissed and surly. I fight my way to my destination, finally arriving in bad mood, militant black woman, cranky feminazi.)

When Yeltsin blared rock music at his opponents holed up in the parliament building in Moscow, in imitation of the U.S. Marines trying to torture Manuel Noriega in Panama, all I could think of was that it must be like being trapped in a crowded subway car when all the portable stereos are tuned to Bob Grant or Howard Stern. With Howard Stern's voice a tinny, screeching backdrop, with all the faces growing dreamily mean as though some soporifically evil hallucinogen were gushing into their bloodstreams, I'd start begging to surrender.

Surrender to what? Surrender to the laissez-faire resegregation that is the metaphoric significance of the hundreds of "Rush rooms" that have cropped up in restaurants around the country; rooms broadcasting Limbaugh's words, rooms for your listening pleasure, rooms where bigots can capture the purity of a Rush-only lunch counter, rooms where all those unpleasant others just "choose" not to eat? Surrender to the naughty luxury of a room in which a Ku Klux Klan meeting could take place in orderly, First Amendment fashion? Everyone's "free" to come in (and a few of you outsiders do), but mostly the undesirable nonconformists are gently repulsed away. It's a high-tech world of enhanced choice. Whites choose mostly to sit in the Rush room. Feminists, blacks, lesbians, and gays "choose" to sit elsewhere. No need to buy black votes, you just pay them not to vote; no need to insist on white-only schools, you just sell the desirability of black-only schools. Just sit back and watch it work, like those invisible shock shields that keep dogs cowering in their own backyards.

How real is the driving perception behind all the Sturm und Drang of this genre of radio-harangue—the perception that white men are an oppressed minority, with no power and no opportunity in the land that they made great? While it is true that power and opportunity are shrinking for all but the very wealthy in this country (and would that Limbaugh would take that issue on), the fact remains that white men are still this country's most privileged citizens and market actors. To give just a small example, according to the *Wall Street Journal,* blacks were the only racial group to suffer a net job loss during the 1990–91 economic downturn at the companies reporting to the Equal Employment Opportunity Commission. Whites, Latinos, and Asians, meanwhile, gained thousands of jobs. While whites gained 71,144 jobs at these companies, Latinos gained 60,040, Asians gained 55,104, and blacks lost 59,479. If every black were hired in the United States tomorrow, the numbers would not be sufficient to account for white men's expanding balloon of fear that they have been specifically dispossessed by African Americans.

25   Given deep patterns of social segregation and general ignorance   25 of history, particularly racial history, media remain the principal source of most Americans' knowledge of each other. Media can provoke violence or induce passivity. In San Francisco, for example, a radio show on KMEL called "Street Soldiers" has taken this power as a responsibility with great consequence: "Unquestionably," writes Ken Auletta in *The New Yorker,* "the show has helped avert violence. When a Samoan teenager was slain, apparently by Filipino gang members, in a drive-by shooting, the phones lit up with calls from Samoans wanting to tell [the hosts] they would not rest until they had exacted revenge. Threats filled the air for a couple of weeks. Then the dead Samoan's father called in, and, in a poignant exchange, the father said he couldn't tolerate the thought of more young men senselessly slaughtered. There would be no retaliation, he vowed. And there was none." In contrast, we must wonder at the phenomenon of the very powerful leadership of the Republican party, from Ronald Reagan to Robert Dole to William Bennett, giving advice, counsel, and friendship to Rush Limbaugh's passionate divisiveness.

The outright denial of the material crisis at every level of U.S. society, most urgently in black inner-city neighborhoods but facing us all, is a kind of political circus, dissembling as it feeds the frustrations of the moment. We as a nation can no longer afford to deal with such crises by *imagining* an excess of bodies, of babies, of job-stealers, of welfare mothers, of overreaching immigrants, of too-powerful (Jewish, in whispers) liberal Hollywood, of lesbians and gays, of gang members ("gangsters" remain white, and no matter what the atrocity, less vilified than "gang members," who are black), of Arab terrorists, and uppity women. The reality of our social poverty far exceeds these scapegoats. This right-wing backlash resembles, in form if not substance, phenomena like anti-Semitism in Poland: there aren't but a handful of Jews left in that whole country, but the giant balloon of heated anti-Semitism flourishes apace, Jews blamed for the world's evils.

The overwhelming response to right-wing excesses in the United States has been to seek an odd sort of comfort in the fact that the First Amendment is working so well that you can't suppress this sort of thing. Look what's happened in Eastern Europe. Granted. So let's not talk about censorship or the First Amendment for the next ten minutes. But in Western Europe, where fascism is rising at an appalling rate, suppression is hardly the problem. In Eastern and Western Europe as well as the United States, we must begin to think just a little bit about the fiercely coalescing power of media to spark mistrust, to fan it into forest fires of fear and revenge. We must begin to think about the levels of national and social complacence in the face of such resolute ignorance. We must ask ourselves what the expected result is, not of censorship or suppression, but of so much encouragement, so much support, so much investment in the fashionability of hate. What future is it that we are designing with the devotion of such tremendous resources to the disgraceful propaganda of bigotry?

Questions on Meaning

1. Explain what specifically offended Williams in the radio conversation she reports.
2. What does Williams suggest is the appeal of "hate" radio to its primary audience—young, white males? What are the negative social effects of this kind of radio program?
3. Is Williams suggesting that hate radio should be censored? What actions does she seem to endorse to combat its messages?

Questions on Rhetorical Strategy and Style

1. The radio programs Williams objects to are politically conservative in their orientation. Does Williams seem like a political liberal who is attacking the programs for partisan reasons? Do her political leanings affect the persuasiveness of her message?
2. Did any of Williams's opinions annoy you? Did any cause you to react with enthusiastic agreement? Explain.
3. Re-examine the third paragraph from the end of the article, the one beginning "Given deep patterns of social segregation and general ignorance. . . ." Evaluate the paragraph's effectiveness in conveying Willliams's central point.

Writing Assignments

1. Tune in to Rush Limbaugh, Howard Stern, Dr. Laura or some other conservative commentators. Listen and take notes (or tape-record) the program and analyze its attitudes. Who does the program host attack? Who is defended? What examples of language might offend certain parties? Write an essay that evaluates Williams's idea that there is a connection between political conservatism and hatred.
2. Look up the first amendment to the Constitution. Then research recent freedom of speech cases such as the People vs. Larry Flynt and the debates on prayer in the schools. In an essay, discuss the definition of the right to freedom of speech including appropriate restraints on that right.

FROM SILENCE TO WORDS:
WRITING AS STRUGGLE

Min-zhan Lu

Min-zhan Lu (1946–) was born in China. Lu, who grew up speaking English as well as a number of Chinese dialects, has taught composition and literary criticism at Drake University. She has published both academic articles related to composition issues and articles about her life in China. This article, published in College English *in 1987, relates Lu's challenges acquiring literacy in both China and the United States and how those challenges have affected her writing and teaching.*

Imagine that you enter a parlor. You come late. When you arrive, others have long preceded you, and they are engaged in a heated discussion. . . .You listen for a while, until you decide that you have caught the tenor of the argument; then you put in your oar. Someone answers; you answer him; another comes to your defense; another aligns himself against you, to either the embarrassment or gratification of your opponent, depending upon the quality of your ally's assistance. However, the discussion is interminable. The hour grows late, you must depart. And you do depart, with the discussion still vigorously in progress.

—*Kenneth Burke, The Philosophy of Literary Form*

Men are not built in silence, but in word, in work, in action-reflection.

—*Paulo Freire, Pedagogy of the Oppressed*

---

1 My mother withdrew into silence two months before she died. A few nights before she fell silent, she told me she regretted the way she had raised me and my sisters. I knew she was referring to the way we had been brought up in the midst of two conflicting worlds—the world of home, dominated by the ideology of the Western humanistic tradition, and the world of a society dominated by Mao Tse-tung's Marxism. My mother had devoted her life to our education, an education she knew had made us suffer political persecution during the Cultural Revolution. I wanted to find a way to convince her that, in spite of the persecution, I had benefited from the education she had worked so hard to give me. But I was silent. My understanding of my education was so dominated by memories of confusion and frustration that I was unable to reflect on what I could have gained from it.

This paper is my attempt to fill up that silence with words, words I didn't have then, words that I have since come to by reflecting on my earlier experience as a student in China and on my recent experience as a composition teacher in the United States. For in spite of the frustration and confusion I experienced growing up caught between two conflicting worlds, the conflict ultimately helped me to grow as a reader and writer. Constantly having to switch back and forth between the discourse of home and that of school made me sensitive and self-conscious about the struggle I experienced every time I tried to read, write, or think in either discourse. Eventually, it led me to search for constructive uses for such struggle.

From early childhood, I had identified the differences between home and the outside world by the different languages I used in each. My parents had wanted my sisters and me to get the best education they could conceive of—Cambridge. They had hired a live-in tutor, a Scot, to make us bilingual. I learned to speak English with my parents, my tutor, and my sisters. I was allowed to speak Shanghai dialect only with the servants. When I was four (the year after the Communist Revolution of 1949), my parents sent me to a local private school where I learned to speak, read, and write in a new language—Standard Chinese, the official written language of New China.

In those days I moved from home to school, from English to Standard Chinese to Shanghai dialect, with no apparent friction. I spoke each language with those who spoke the language. All seemed quite "natural"—servants spoke only Shanghai dialect because they were servants; teachers spoke Standard Chinese because they were teachers; languages had different words because they were different languages. I thought of English as my family language, comparable to the many strange dialects I didn't speak but had often heard some of my classmates speak with their families. While I was happy to have a special family language, until second grade I didn't feel that my family language was any different than some of my classmates' family dialects.

My second grade homeroom teacher was a young graduate from a missionary school. When she found out I spoke English, she began to practice her English on me. One day she used English when asking me to run an errand for her. As I turned to close the door behind me, I noticed the puzzled faces of my classmates. I had the same sensation I had often experienced when some stranger in a crowd would turn on hearing me speak English. I was more intensely pleased on this occasion, however, because suddenly I felt that my family language had been singled out from the family languages of my classmates. Since we were not allowed to speak any dialect other than Standard Chinese in the classroom, having my teacher speak English to me in class made English an official language of the classroom. I began to take pride in my ability to speak it.

This incident confirmed in my mind what my parents had always told me about the importance of English to one's life. Time and again they had told me of how my paternal grandfather, who was well versed in classic Chinese, kept losing good-paying jobs because he couldn't speak English. My grandmother reminisced constantly about how she had slaved and saved to send my father to a first-rate missionary school. And we were made to understand that it was my father's fluent English that had opened the door to his success. Even though my family had always stressed the importance of English for my future, I used to complain bitterly about the extra English lessons we had to take after school. It was only after my homeroom teacher had "sanctified" English that I began to connect English with my education. I became a much more eager student in my tutorials.

What I learned from my tutorials seemed to enhance and reinforce what I was learning in my classroom. In those days each word had one meaning. One day I would be making a sentence at school: "The national flag of China is red." The next day I would recite at home, "My love is like a red, red rose." There seemed to be an agreement between the Chinese "red" and the English "red," and both corresponded to the patch of color printed next to the word. "Love" was my love for my mother at home and my love for my "motherland" at school; both "loves" meant how I felt about my mother. Having two loads of homework forced me to develop a quick memory for words and a sensitivity to form and style. What I learned in one language carried over to the other. I made sentences such as, "I saw a red, red rose among the green leaves," with both the English lyric and the classic Chinese lyric—red flower among green leaves—running through my mind, and I was praised by both teacher and tutor for being a good student.

Although my elementary schooling took place during the fifties, I was almost oblivious to the great political and social changes happening around me. Years later, I read in my history and political philosophy textbooks that the fifties were a time when "China was making a transition from a semi-feudal, semi-capitalist, and semi-colonial country into a socialist country," a period in which "the Proletarians were breaking into the educational territory dominated by Bourgeois Intellectuals." While people all over the country were being officially classified into Proletarians, Petty-bourgeois, National-bourgeois, Poor-peasants, and Intellectuals, and were trying to adjust to their new social identities, my parents were allowed to continue the upper middle-class life they had established before the 1949 Revolution because of my father's affiliation with British firms. I had always felt that my family was different from the families of my classmates, but I didn't perceive society's view of my family until the summer vacation before I entered high school.

First, my aunt was caught by her colleagues talking to her husband over the phone in English. Because of it, she was criticized and almost labeled a Rightist. (This was the year of the Anti-Rightist movement, a movement in which the Intellectuals became the target of the "socialist class-struggle.") I had heard others telling my mother that she was foolish to teach us English when Russian had replaced English as the "official" foreign language. I had also learned at school that the American and British Imperialists were the arch-enemies of New China. Yet I had made no connection between the arch-enemies and the English our family spoke. What happened to my aunt forced the connection on me. I began to see my parents' choice of a family language as an anti-Revolutionary act and was alarmed that I had participated in such an act. From then on, I took care not to use English outside home and to conceal my knowledge of English from my new classmates.

Certain words began to play important roles in my new life at the junior high. On the first day of school, we were handed forms to fill out with our parents' class, job, and income. Being one of the few people not employed by the government, my father had never been officially classified. Since he was a medical doctor, he told me to put him down as an Intellectual. My homeroom teacher called me into the office a couple of days afterwards and told me that my father couldn't be an Intellectual if his income far exceeded that of a Capitalist. He also told me that since my father worked for Foreign Imperialists, my father should be classified as an Imperialist Lackey. The teacher looked nonplussed when I told him that my father couldn't be an Imperialist Lackey because he was a medical doctor. But I could tell from the way he took notes on my form that my father's job had put me in an unfavorable position in his eyes.

The Standard Chinese term "class" was not a new word for me. Since first grade, I had been taught sentences such as, "The Working class are the masters of New China." I had always known that it was good to be a worker, but until then, I had never felt threatened for not being one. That fall, "class" began to take on a new meaning for me. I noticed a group of Working-class students and teachers at school. I was made to understand that because of my class background, I was excluded from that group.

Another word that became important was "consciousness." One of the slogans posted in the school building read, "Turn our students into future Proletarians with socialist consciousness and education!" For several weeks we studied this slogan in our political philosophy course, a subject I had never had in elementary school. I still remember the definition of "socialist consciousness" that we were repeatedly tested on through the years: "Socialist consciousness is a person's political soul. It is the consciousness of the Proletarians represented by Marxist Mao Tse-tung thought. It takes expression in one's action, language, and lifestyle. It is the task of every Chinese student to grow up into a Proletarian with a socialist consciousness so that he can serve the people and the motherland." To make the abstract concept accessible to us, our teacher pointed out that the immediate task for students from Working-class families was to strengthen their socialist consciousnesses. For those of us who were from other class backgrounds, the task was to turn ourselves into Workers with socialist consciousnesses. The teacher never explained exactly how we were supposed to "turn" into Workers. Instead, we were given samples of the ritualistic annual plans we had to write at the beginning of each term. In these plans, we performed "self-criticism" on our consciousnesses and made vows to turn ourselves into Workers with socialist consciousnesses. The teacher's division between those who did and those who didn't have a socialist consciousness led me to reify the notion of "consciousness" into a thing one possesses. I equated this intangible "thing" with a concrete way of dressing, speaking, and writing. For instance, I never doubted that my political philosophy teacher had a socialist consciousness because she was from a steelworker's family (she announced this the first day of class) and was a party member who wore grey cadre suits and talked like a philosophy textbook. I noticed other things about her. She had beautiful eyes and spoke Standard Chinese with such a pure accent that I thought she should be a film star. But I was embarrassed that I had noticed things that ought not to have been associated with her. I blamed my observation on my Bourgeois consciousness.

At the same time, the way reading and writing were taught through memorization and imitation also encouraged me to reduce concepts and ideas to simple definitions. In literature and political philosophy classes, we were taught a large number of quotations from Marx, Lenin, and Mao Tse-tung. Each concept that appeared in these quotations came with a definition. We were required to memorize the definitions of the words along with the quotations. Every time I memorized a definition, I felt I had learned a word: "The national red flag symbolizes the blood shed by Revolutionary ancestors for our socialist cause"; "New China rises like a red sun over the eastern horizon." As I memorized these sentences, I reduced their metaphors to dictionary meanings: "red" meant "Revolution" and "red sun" meant "New China" in the "language" of the Working class. I learned mechanically but eagerly. I soon became quite fluent in this new language.

As school began to define me as a political subject, my parents tried to build up my resistance to the "communist poisoning" by exposing me to the "great books"—novels by Charles Dickens, Nathaniel Hawthorne, Emily Brontë, Jane Austen, and writers from around the turn of the century. My parents implied that these writers represented how I, their child, should read and write. My parents replaced the word "Bourgeois" with the word "cultured." They reminded me that I was in school only to learn math and science. I needed to pass the other courses to stay in school, but I was not to let the "Red doctrines" corrupt my mind. Gone were the days when I could innocently write, "I saw the red, red rose among the green leaves," collapsing, as I did, English and Chinese cultural traditions. "Red" came to mean Revolution at school, "the Commies" at home, and adultery in *The Scarlet Letter.* Since I took these symbols and metaphors as meanings natural to people of the same class, I abandoned my earlier definitions of English and Standard Chinese as the language of home and the language of school. I now defined English as the language of the Bourgeois and Standard Chinese as the language of the Working class. I thought of the language of the Working class as someone else's language and the language of the Bourgeois as my language. But I also believed that, although the language of the Bourgeois was my real language, I could and would adopt the language of the Working class when I was at school. I began to put on and take off my Working class language in the same way I put on and took off my school clothes to avoid being criticized for wearing Bourgeois clothes.

15   In my literature classes, I learned the Working-class formula for reading. Each work in the textbook had a short "Author's Biography": "X X X, born in 19—in the province of X X X, is from a Worker's family. He joined the Revolution in 19—. He is a Revolutionary realist with a passionate love for the Party and Chinese Revolution. His work expresses the thoughts and emotions of the masses and sings praise to the prosperous socialist construction on all fronts of China." The teacher used the "Author's Biography" as a yardstick to measure the texts. We were taught to locate details in the texts that illustrated these summaries, such as words that expressed Workers' thoughts and emotions or events that illustrated the Workers' lives.

I learned a formula for Working-class writing in the composition classes. We were given sample essays and told to imitate them. The theme was always about how the collective taught the individual a lesson. I would write papers about labor-learning experiences or school-cleaning days, depending on the occasion of the collective activity closest to the assignment. To make each paper look different, I dressed it up with details about the date, the weather, the environment, or the appearance of the Master-worker who had taught me "the lesson." But as I became more and more fluent in the generic voice of the Working-class Student, I also became more and more self-conscious about the language we used at home.

For instance, in senior high we began to have English classes ("to study English for the Revolution," as the slogan on the cover of the textbook said), and I was given my first Chinese-English dictionary. There I discovered the English version of the term "class-struggle." (The Chinese characters for a school "class" and for a social "class" are different.) I had often used the English word "class" at home in sentences such as, "So and so has class," but I had not connected this sense of "class" with "class-struggle." Once the connection was made, I heard a second layer of meaning every time someone at home said a person had "class." The expression began to mean the person had the style and sophistication characteristic of the bourgeoisie. The word lost its innocence. I was uneasy about hearing that second layer of meaning because I was sure my parents did not hear the word that way. I felt that therefore I should not be hearing it that way either. Hearing the second layer of meaning made me wonder if I was losing my English.

My suspicion deepened when I noticed myself unconsciously merging and switching between the "reading" of home and the "reading" of school. Once I had to write a report on *The Revolutionary Family*, a book about an illiterate woman's awakening and growth as a Revolutionary through the deaths of her husband and all her children for the cause of the Revolution. In one scene the woman deliberated over whether or not she should encourage her youngest son to join the Revolution. Her memory of her husband's death made her afraid to encourage her son. Yet she also remembered her earlier married life and the first time her husband tried to explain the meaning of the Revolution to her. These memories made her feel she should encourage her son to continue the cause his father had begun.

I was moved by this scene. "Moved" was a word my mother and sisters used a lot when we discussed books. Our favorite moments in novels were moments of what I would now call internal conflict, moments which we said "moved" us. I remember that we were "moved" by Jane Eyre when she was torn between her sense of ethics, which compelled her to leave the man she loved, and her impulse to stay with the only man who had ever loved her. We were also moved by Agnes in *David Copperfield* because of the way she restrained her love for

David so that he could live happily with the woman he loved. My standard method of doing a book report was to model it on the review by the Publishing Bureau and to dress it up with detailed quotations from the book. The review of *The Revolutionary Family* emphasized the woman's Revolutionary spirit. I decided to use the scene that had moved me to illustrate this point. I wrote the report the night before it was due. When I had finished, I realized I couldn't possibly hand it in. Instead of illustrating her Revolutionary spirit, I had dwelled on her internal conflict, which could be seen as a moment of weak sentimentality that I should never have emphasized in a Revolutionary heroine. I wrote another report, taking care to illustrate the grandeur of her Revolutionary spirit by expanding on a quotation in which she decided that if the life of her son could change the lives of millions of sons, she should not begrudge his life for the cause of Revolution. I handed in my second version but kept the first in my desk.

I never showed it to anyone. I could never show it to people outside my family, because it had deviated so much from the reading enacted by the jacket review. Neither could I show it to my mother or sisters, because I was ashamed to have been so moved by such a "Revolutionary" book. My parents would have been shocked to learn that I could like such a book in the same way they liked Dickens. Writing this book report increased my fear that I was losing the command over both the "language of home" and the "language of school" that I had worked so hard to gain. I tried to remind myself that, if I could still tell when my reading or writing sounded incorrect, then I had retained my command over both languages. Yet I could no longer be confident of my command over either language because I had discovered that when I was not careful—or even when I was—my reading and writing often surprised me with its impurity. To prevent such impurity, I became very suspicious of my thoughts when I read or wrote. I was always asking myself why I was using this word, how I was using it, always afraid that I wasn't reading or writing correctly. What confused and frustrated me most was that I could not figure out why I was no longer able to read or write correctly without such painful deliberation.

I continued to read only because reading allowed me to keep my thoughts and confusion private. I hoped that somehow, if I watched myself carefully, I would figure out from the way I read whether I had really mastered the "languages." But writing became a dreadful chore. When I tried to keep a diary, I was so afraid that the voice of school might slip in that I could only list my daily activities. When I wrote for school, I worried that my Bourgeois sensibilities would betray me.

The more suspicious I became about the way I read and wrote, the more guilty I felt for losing the spontaneity with which I had learned to "use" these "languages." Writing the book report made me feel that my reading and writing in the "language" of either home or school could not be free of the interference of the other. But I was unable to acknowledge, grasp, or grapple with what I was experiencing, for both my parents and my teachers had suggested that, if I were a good student, such interference would and should not take place. I assumed that once I had "acquired" a discourse, I could simply switch it on and off every time I read and wrote as I would some electronic tool. Furthermore, I expected my readings and writings to come out in their correct forms whenever I switched the proper discourse on. I still regarded the discourse of home as natural and the discourse of school alien, but I never had doubted before that I could acquire both and switch them on and off according to the occasion.

When my experience in writing conflicted with what I thought should happen when I used each discourse, I rejected my experience because it contradicted what my parents and teachers had taught me. I shied away from writing to avoid what I assumed I should not experience. But trying to avoid what should not happen did not keep it from recurring whenever I had to write. Eventually my confusion and frustration over these recurring experiences compelled me to search for an explanation: how and why had I failed to learn what my parents and teachers had worked so hard to teach me?

I now think of the internal scene for my reading and writing about *The Revolutionary Family* as a heated discussion between myself, the voices of home, and those of school. The review on the back of the book, the sample student papers I came across in my composition classes, my philosophy teacher—these I heard as voices of one group. My parents and my home readings were the voices of an opposing group. But the conversation between these opposing voices in the internal scene of my writing was not as polite and respectful as the parlor scene Kenneth Burke has portrayed (see epigraph). Rather, these voices struggled to dominate the discussion, constantly incorporating, dismissing, or suppressing the arguments of each other, like the battles between the hegemonic and counter-hegemonic forces described in Raymond Williams' *Marxism and Literature* (108–14).

25   When I read *The Revolutionary Family* and wrote the first version   25
of my report, I began with a quotation from the review. The voices of
both home and school answered, clamoring to be heard. I tried to listen to one group and turn a deaf ear to the other. Both persisted. I negotiated my way through these conflicting voices, now agreeing with
one, now agreeing with the other. I formed a reading out of my interaction with both. Yet I was afraid to have done so because both
home and school had implied that I should speak in unison with only
one of these groups and stand away from the discussion rather than
participate in it.

My teachers and parents had persistently called my attention to
the intensity of the discussion taking place on the external social scene.
The story of my grandfather's failure and my father's success had from
my early childhood made me aware of the conflict between Western
and traditional Chinese cultures. My political education at school
added another dimension to the conflict; the war of Marxist-Maoism
against them both. Yet when my parents and teachers called my attention to the conflict, they stressed the anxiety of having to live
through China's transformation from a semi-feudal, semi-capitalist,
and semi-colonial society to a socialist one. Acquiring the discourse of
the dominant group was, to them, a means of seeking alliance with
that group and thus of surviving the whirlpool of cultural currents
around them. As a result, they modeled their pedagogical practices on
this utilitarian view of language. Being the eager student, I adopted
this view of language as a tool for survival. It came to dominate my
understanding of the discussion on the social and historical scene and
to restrict my ability to participate in that discussion.

To begin with, the metaphor of language as a tool for survival led
me to be passive in my use of discourse, to be a bystander in the discussion. In Burke's "parlor," everyone is involved in the discussion. As
it goes on through history, what we call "communal discourses"—arguments specific to particular political, social, economic, ethnic, sexual, and family groups—form, re-form and transform. To use a
discourse in such a scene is to participate in the argument and to contribute to the formation of the discourse. But when I was growing up,
I could not take on the burden of such an active role in the discussion. For both home and school presented the existent conventions of
the discourse each taught me as absolute laws for my action. They
turned verbal action into a tool, a set of conventions produced and

shaped prior to and outside of my own verbal acts. Because I saw language as a tool, I separated the process of producing the tool from the process of using it. The tool was made by someone else and was then acquired and used by me. How the others made it before I acquired it determined and guaranteed what it produced when I used it. I imagined that the more experienced and powerful members of the community were the ones responsible for making the tool. They were the ones who participated in the discussion and fought with opponents. When I used what they made, their labor and accomplishments would ensure the quality of my reading and writing. By using it, I could survive the heated discussion. When my immediate experience in writing the book report suggested that knowing the conventions of school did not guarantee the form and content of my report, when it suggested that I had to write the report with the work and responsibility I had assigned to those who wrote book reviews in the Publishing bureau, I thought I had lost the tool I had earlier acquired.

Another reason I could not take up an active role in the argument was that my parents and teachers contrived to provide a scene free of conflict for practicing my various languages. It was as if their experience had made them aware of the conflict between their discourse and other discourses and of the struggle involved in reproducing the conventions of any discourse on a scene where more than one discourse exists. They seemed convinced that such conflict and struggle would overwhelm someone still learning the discourse. Home and school each contrived a purified space where only one discourse was spoken and heard. In their choice of textbooks, in the way they spoke, and in the way they required me to speak, each jealously silenced any voice that threatened to break the unison of the scene. The homogeneity of home and of school implied that only one discourse could and should be relevant in each place. It led me to believe I should leave behind, turn a deaf ear to, or forget the discourse of the other when I crossed the boundary dividing them. I expected myself to set down one discourse whenever I took up another just as I would take off or put on a particular set of clothes for school or home.

Despite my parents' and teachers' attempts to keep home and school discrete, the internal conflict between the two discourses continued whenever I read or wrote. Although I tried to suppress the voice of one discourse in the name of the other, having to speak aloud in the voice I had just silenced each time I crossed the boundary kept both voices active in my mind. Every "I think . . . " from the voice of home or school brought forth a "However . . . " or a "But. . ." from the voice of the opponents. To identify with the voice of home or school, I had to negotiate through the conflicting voices of both by restating, taking back, qualifying my thoughts. I was unconsciously doing so when I did my book report. But I could not use the interaction comfortably and constructively. Both my parents and my teachers had implied that my job was to prevent that interaction from happening. My sense of having failed to accomplish what they had taught silenced me.

To use the interaction between the discourses of home and school constructively, I would have to have seen reading or writing as a process in which I worked my way towards a stance through a dialectical process of identification and division. To identify with an ally, I would have to have grasped the distance between where he or she stood and where I was positioning myself. In taking a stance against an opponent, I would have to have grasped where my stance identified with the stance of my allies. Teetering along the "wavering line of pressure and counter-pressure" from both allies and opponents, I might have worked my way towards a stance of my own (Burke, *A Rhetoric of Motives,* 23). Moreover, I would have to have understood that the voices in my mind, like the participants in the parlor scene, were in constant flux. As I came into contact with new and different groups of people or read different books, voices entered and left. Each time I read or wrote, the stance I negotiated out of these voices would always be at some distance from the stances I worked out in my previous and my later readings or writings.

I could not conceive such a form of action for myself because I saw reading and writing as an expression of an established stance. In delineating the conventions of a discourse, my parents and teachers had synthesized the stance they saw as typical for a representative member of the community. Burke calls this the stance of a "god" or the "prototype"; Williams calls it the "official" or "possible" stance of the community. Through the metaphor of the survival tool, my parents and teachers had led me to assume I could automatically reproduce the official stance of the discourse I used. Therefore, when I did my book report on *The Revolutionary Family,* I expected my knowledge of the official stance set by the book review to ensure the actual stance of my report. As it happened, I began by trying to take the official stance of the review. Other voices interrupted. I answered back. In the process, I worked out a stance approximate but not identical to the official stance I began with. Yet the experience of having to labor to realize my knowledge of the official stance or to prevent myself from wandering away from it frustrated and confused me. For even though I had been actually reading and writing in a Burkean scene, I was afraid to participate actively in the discussion. I assumed it was my role to survive by staying out of it.

Not long ago, my daughter told me that it bothered her to hear her friend "talk wrong." Having come to the United States from China with little English, my daughter has become sensitive to the way English, as spoken by her teachers, operates. As a result, she has amazed her teachers with her success in picking up the language and in adapting to life at school. Her concern to speak the English taught in the classroom "correctly" makes her uncomfortable when she hears people using "ain't" or double negatives, which her teacher considers "improper." I see in her the me that had eagerly learned and used the discourse of the Working class at school. Yet while I was torn between the two conflicting worlds of school and home, she moves with seeming ease from the conversations she hears over the dinner table to her teacher's words in the classroom. My husband and I are proud of the good work she does at school. We are glad she is spared the kinds of conflict between home and school I experienced at her age. Yet as we watch her becoming more and more fluent in the language of the classroom, we wonder if, by enabling her to "survive" school, her very fluency will silence her when the scene of her reading and writing expands beyond that of the composition classroom.

For when I listen to my daughter, to students, and to some composition teachers talking about the teaching and learning of writing, I am often alarmed by the degree to which the metaphor of a survival tool dominates their understanding of language as it once dominated my own. I am especially concerned with the way some composition classes focus on turning the classroom into a monological scene for the students' reading and writing. Most of our students live in a world similar to my daughter's, somewhere between the purified world of the classroom and the complex world of my adolescence. When composition classes encourage these students to ignore those voices that seem irrelevant to the purified world of the classroom, most students are often able to do so without much struggle. Some of them are so adept at doing it that the whole process has for them become automatic.

However, beyond the classroom and beyond the limited range of these students' immediate lives lies a much more complex and dynamic social and historical scene. To help these students become actors in such a scene, perhaps we need to call their attention to voices that may seem irrelevant to the discourse we teach rather than encourage them to shut them out. For example, we might intentionally complicate the classroom scene by bringing into it discourses that stand at varying distances from the one we teach. We might encourage students to explore ways of practicing the conventions of the discourse they are learning by negotiating through these conflicting voices. We could also encourage them to see themselves as responsible for forming or transforming as well as preserving the discourse they are learning.

35 As I think about what we might do to complicate the external and internal scenes of our students' writing, I hear my parents and teachers saying: "Not now. Keep them from the wrangle of the marketplace until they have acquired the discourse and are skilled at using it." And I answer: "Don't teach them to 'survive' the whirlpool of crosscurrents by avoiding it. Use the classroom to moderate the currents. Moderate the currents, but teach them from the beginning to struggle." When I think of the ways in which the teaching of reading and writing as classroom activities can frustrate the development of students, I am almost grateful for the overwhelming complexity of the circumstances in which I grew up. For it was this complexity that kept me from losing sight of the effort and choice involved in reading or writing with and through a discourse.

References

Burke, Kenneth. *The Philosophy of Literary Form: Studies in Symbolic Action.* 2nd ed. Baton Rouge: Louisiana State UP, 1967.

———. *A Rhetoric of Motives.* Berkeley: U of California P, 1969.

Freire, Paulo. *Pedagogy of the Oppressed.* Trans. M. B. Ramos. New York: Continuum, 1970.

Williams, Raymond. *Marxism and Literature.* New York: Oxford UP, 1977.

Questions on Meaning

1. What were the two conflicting worlds in which Lu grew up? What were the "two discourses" of these worlds? How did these "two discourses" create tension in her life? Why did her mother regret bringing her up in these conflicting worlds?
2. What did Lu consider her "family language"? How did her perception of her "family language" change as she learned more about *class* in her society? Why did she become alarmed at her family's use of that language?
3. How did the metaphor of "language as a tool" cause Lu to become passive in her discourse?
4. Reread the section where Lu compares and contrasts her first and second versions of her book review of *The Revolutionary Family.* Why did her first version trouble her so? Why could she not show it to anyone outside her family? How did this experience affect her reading and writing—notably her writing in her diary?

Questions on Rhetorical Strategy and Style

1. How does Lu use a cause and effect writing strategy to relate the two worlds in which she lived as a child to her development as a reader and writer? What was the effect of the two loads of homework Lu carried, one from her English tutor, one from her Chinese teachers? What was the effect of her Chinese teachers' requirement that she learn reading and writing through memorization and imitation?
2. Lu uses the words "class" and "consciousness" as examples of words that "began to play important roles in my new life at the junior high." How did the word "class" make her feel different? Why did the word "consciousness" create confusion in her life?

Writing Assignments

1. Describe a time when you were afraid to reveal something you had written because it deviated from what was expected. What made it unacceptable? Why had you written it? Ultimately, what did you do with it?
2. Learn more about Kenneth Burke. Why are his theories important to Lu's argument? Why did she become a "bystander" in his "parlor"?

3. Write an essay about a time when you used language as a tool, such as through word choice, diction, and maybe even accent. (Perhaps you were putting on airs to impress someone, trying to sound like a regular Joe to hide your education, or talking slowly and methodically to someone who does not have strong command of English.) Who was the audience? What was the result of your use of language as a tool? Explain why language is or is not an effective communications tool for you.

⌒ HOW TO TAME ⌒
A WILD TONGUE

Gloria Anzaldúa

Gloria Anzaldúa (1942–2004), a Mexican-American feminist writer, grew up in southwest Texas. The author of Borderlands/La Frontera: The New Mestiza *(1987), she also edited two volumes of minority women's writing,* This Bridge Called My Back: Writing by Radical Women of Color *(1983) and* Hacienda Caras: Making Face/ Making Soul *(1990). Anzaldúa also wrote two children's books,* Friends from the Other Side/Amigos del Otro Lado *(1993) and* Prietita and the Ghost Woman/ Prietita y la Llorona *(1995), in addition to a memoir-like collection of interviews titled* Interviews/Ientrevistas *(2000). In this essay, a chapter from* Borderlands, *Anzaldúa describes the history and vital importance of her language and its many variations.*

1 "We're going to have to control your tongue," the dentist says, pulling out all the metal from my mouth. Silver bits plop and tinkle into the basin. My mouth is a motherlode.

The dentist is cleaning out my roots. I get a whiff of the stench when I gasp. "I can't cap that tooth yet, you're still draining," he says.

"We're going to have to do something about your tongue," I hear the anger rising in his voice. My tongue keeps pushing out the wads of cotton, pushing back the drills, the long thin needles. "I've never seen anything as strong or as stubborn," he says. And I think, how do you tame a wild tongue, train it to be quiet, how do you bridle and saddle it? How do you make it lie down?

"Who is to say that robbing a people of
its language is less violent than war?"
—Ray Gwyn Smith[1]

I remember being caught speaking Spanish at recess—that was
good for three licks on the knuckles with a sharp ruler. I remember
being sent to the corner of the classroom for "talking back" to the
Anglo teacher when all I was trying to do was tell her how to pronounce my name. "If you want to be American, speak 'American.' If
you don't like it, go back to Mexico where you belong."

"I want you to speak English. *Pa' hallar buen trabajo tienes que
saber hablar el inglés bien. Qué vale toda tu educación si todavía hables
inglés con un 'accent,'* " my mother would say, mortified that I spoke
English like a Mexican. At Pan American University, I, and all Chicano students, were required to take two speech classes. Their purpose:
to get rid of our accents.

Attacks on one's form of expression with the intent to censor
are a violation of the First Amendment. *El Anglo con cara de inocente
nos arrancó la lengua.* Wild tongues can't be tamed, they can only be
cut out.

Overcoming the Tradition of Silence

*Ahogadas, escupimos el oscuro.
Peleando con nuestra propia sombra
el silencio nos sepulta.*

En boca cerrada no entran moscas. "Flies don't enter a closed
mouth" is a saying I kept hearing when I was a child. *Ser habladora*
was to be a gossip and a liar, to talk too much. *Muchachitas bien cri-
adas,* well-bred girls, don't answer back. *Es una falta de respeto* to talk
back to one's mother or father. I remember one of the sins I'd recite
to the priest in the confession box the few times I went to confession:
talking back to my mother, *hablar pa' 'tras, replar. Hocicona, repelona,
chismosa,* having a big mouth, questioning, carrying tales are all signs
of being *mal criada.* In my culture they are all words that are deroga-
tory if applied to women—I've never heard them applied to men.

---

[1]Ray Gwyn Smith, *Moorland Is Cold Country,* unpublished book.

The first time I heard two women, a Puerto Rican and a Cuban, say the word *"nosotras,"* I was shocked. I had not known the word existed. Chicanos use *nosotros* whether we're male or female. We are robbed of our female being by the masculine plural. Language is a male discourse.

> And our tongues have become
> dry   the wilderness has
> dried out our tongues   and
> we have forgotten speech.
> —Irena Klepfisz[2]

Even our own people, other Spanish speakers *nos quieren poner candados en la boca.* They would hold us back with their bag of *reglas de academia.*

Oyé como ladra: el lenguaje de la frontera

Quien tiene boca se equivoca.
—Mexican saying

"Pocho, cultural traitor, you're speaking the oppressor's language by speaking English, you're ruining the Spanish language," I have been accused by various Latinos and Latinas. Chicano Spanish is considered by the purist and by most Latinos deficient, a mutilation of Spanish.

But Chicano Spanish is a border tongue which developed naturally. Change, *evolución, enriquecimiento de palabras nuevas por invención o adopción* have created variants of Chicano Spanish, *un nuevo lenguaje. Un lenguaje que corresponde a un modo de vivir.* Chicano Spanish is not incorrect; it is a living language.

For a people who are neither Spanish nor live in a country in which Spanish is the first language; for a people who live in a country in which English is the reigning tongue but who are not Anglo; for a people who cannot identify with either standard (formal, Castilian) Spanish nor standard English, what recourse is left to them but to create their own

---

[2]Irena Klepfisz, *"Di rayze aheym/*The Journey Home," in *The Tribe of Dina: A Jewish Women's Anthology,* Melanie Kaye/Kantrowitz and Irena Klepfisz, eds. (Montpelier, VT: Sinister Wisdom Books, 1986), 49.

language? A language which they can connect their identity to, one capable of communicating the realities and values true to themselves— a language with terms that are neither *español ni inglés,* but both. We speak a *patois,* a forked tongue, a variation of two languages.

Chicano Spanish sprang out of the Chicanos' need to identify ourselves as a distinct people. We needed a language with which we could communicate with ourselves, a secret language. For some of us, language is a homeland closer than the Southwest—for many Chicanos today live in the Midwest and the East. And because we are a complex, heterogeneous people, we speak many languages. Some of the languages we speak are:

1. Standard English
2. Working class and slang English
3. Standard Spanish
4. Standard Mexican Spanish
5. North Mexican Spanish dialect
6. Chicano Spanish (Texas, New Mexico, Arizona and California have regional variations)
7. Tex-Mex
8. *Pachuco* (called *caló*)

My "home" tongues are the languages I speak with my sister and brothers, with my friends. They are the last five listed, with 6 and 7 being closest to my heart. From school, the media and job situations, I've picked up standard and working class English. From Mamagrande Locha and from reading Spanish and Mexican literature, I've picked up Standard Spanish and Standard Mexican Spanish. From *los recién llegados,* Mexican immigrants, and *braceros,* I learned the North Mexican dialect. With Mexicans I'll try to speak either Standard Mexican Spanish or the North Mexican dialect. From my parents and Chicanos living in the Valley, I picked up Chicano Texas Spanish, and I speak it with my mom, younger brother (who married a Mexican and who rarely mixes Spanish with English), and aunts and older relatives.

15   With Chicanas from *Nuevo México* or *Arizona* I will speak Chi-   15
cano Spanish a little, but often they don't understand what I'm saying. With most California Chicanas I speak entirely in English (unless I forget). When I first moved to San Francisco, I'd rattle off something in Spanish, unintentionally embarrassing them. Often it is only with another Chicana *tejana* that I can talk freely.

Words distorted by English are known as anglicisms or *pochismos*. The *pocho* is an anglicized Mexican or American of Mexican origin who speaks Spanish with an accent characteristic of North Americans and who distorts and reconstructs the language according to the influence of English.[3] Tex-Mex, or Spanglish, comes most naturally to me. I may switch back and forth from English to Spanish in the same sentence or in the same word. With my sister and my brother Nune and with Chicano *tejano* contemporaries I speak in Tex-Mex.

From kids and people my own age I picked up *Pachuco*. Pachuco (the language of the zoot suiters) is a language of rebellion, both against Standard Spanish and Standard English. It is a secret language. Adults of the culture and outsiders cannot understand it. It is made up of slang words from both English and Spanish. *Ruca* means girl or woman, *vato* means guy or dude, *chale* means no, *simón* means yes, *churro* is sure, talk is *periquiar, pigionear* means petting, *qué gacho* means how nerdy, *ponte águila* means watch out, death is called *la pelona*. Through lack of practice and not having others who can speak it, I've lost most of the *Pachuco* tongue.

Chicano Spanish

Chicanos, after 250 years of Spanish/Anglo colonization, have developed significant differences in the Spanish we speak. We collapse two adjacent vowels into a single syllable and sometimes shift the stress in certain words such as *maíz/maiz, cohete/cuete*. We leave out certain consonants when they appear between vowels: *lado/lao, mojado/mojao*. Chicanos from South Texas pronounce *f* as *j* as in *jue (fue)*. Chicanos use "archaisms," words that are no longer in the Spanish language, words that have been evolved out. We say *semos, truje, haiga, ansina*, and *naiden*. We retain the "archaic" *j*, as in *jalar*, that derives from an earlier *h*, (the French *halar* or the Germanic *halon* which was lost to standard Spanish in the 16th century), but which is still found in several regional dialects such as the one spoken in South Texas. (Due to geography, Chicanos from the Valley of South Texas were cut off linguistically from other Spanish speakers. We tend to use words that the Spaniards brought over from Medieval Spain. The majority of the

---

[3] R. C. Ortega, *Dialectología Del Barrio*, trans. Hortencia S. Alwan (Los Angeles, CA: R. C. Ortega Publisher & Bookseller, 1977), 132.

Spanish colonizers in Mexico and the Southwest came from Extremadura—Hernán Cortés was one of them—and Andalucía. Andalucians pronounce *ll* like a *y,* and their *d*'s tend to be absorbed by adjacent vowels: *tirado* becomes *tirao.* They brought *el lenguaje popular, dialectos y regionalismos.*[4])

Chicanos and other Spanish speakers also shift *ll* to *y* and *z* to *s.*[5] We leave out initial syllables, saying *tar* for *estar, toy* for *estoy, hora* for *ahora* (*cubanos* and *puertorriqueños* also leave out initial letters of some words.) We also leave out the final syllable such as *pa* for *para.* The intervocalic *y,* the *ll* as in *tortilla, ella, botella,* gets replaced by *tortia* or *tortiya, ea, botea.* We add an additional syllable at the beginning of certain words: *atocar* for *tocar, agastar* for *gastar.* Sometimes we'll say *lavaste las vacijas,* other times *lavates* (substituting the *ates* verb endings for the *aste*).

20   We use anglicisms, words borrowed from English: *bola* from ball, *carpeta* from carpet, *máchina de lavar* (instead of *lavadora*) from washing machine. Tex-Mex argot, created by adding a Spanish sound at the beginning or end of an English word such as *cookiar* for cook, *watchiar* for watch, *parkiar* for park, and *rapiar* for rape, is the result of the pressures on Spanish speakers to adapt to English.   20

We don't use the word *vosotros/as* or its accompanying verb form. We don't say *claro* (to mean yes), *imagínate,* or *me emociona,* unless we picked up Spanish from Latinas, out of a book, or in a classroom. Other Spanish-speaking groups are going through the same, or similar, development in their Spanish.

Linguistic Terrorism

> *Deslenguadas. Somos los del español deficiente.* We are your linguistic nightmare, your linguistic aberration, your linguistic *mestisaje,* the subject of your *burla.* Because we speak with tongues of fire we are culturally crucified. Racially, culturally and linguistically *somos huérfanos*—we speak an orphan tongue.

Chicanas who grew up speaking Chicano Spanish have internalized the belief that we speak poor Spanish. It is illegitimate, a bastard

---

[4]Eduardo Hernández-Chávez, Andrew D. Cohen, and Anthony F. Beltramo, *El Lenguaje de los Chicanos: Regional and Social Characteristics Used By Mexican Americans* (Arlington, VA: Center for Applied Linguistics, 1975), 39.

[5]Hernández-Chávez, xvii.

language. And because we internalize how our language has been used against us by the dominant culture, we use our language differences against each other.

Chicana feminists often skirt around each other with suspicion and hesitation. For the longest time I couldn't figure it out. Then it dawned on me. To be close to another Chicana is like looking into the mirror. We are afraid of what we'll see there. *Pena.* Shame. Low estimation of self. In childhood we are told that our language is wrong. Repeated attacks on our native tongue diminish our sense of self. The attacks continue throughout our lives.

Chicanas feel uncomfortable talking in Spanish to Latinas, afraid of their censure. Their language was not outlawed in their countries. They had a whole lifetime of being immersed in their native tongue; generations, centuries in which Spanish was a first language, taught in school, heard on radio and TV, and read in the newspaper.

25   If a person, Chicana or Latina, has a low estimation of my native 25
tongue, she also has a low estimation of me. Often with *mexicanas y latinas* we'll speak English as a neutral language. Even among Chicanas we tend to speak English at parties or conferences. Yet, at the same time, we're afraid the other will think we're *agringadas* because we don't speak Chicano Spanish. We oppress each other trying to out-Chicano each other, vying to be the "real" Chicanas, to speak like Chicanos. There is no one Chicano language just as there is no one Chicano experience. A monolingual Chicana whose first language is English or Spanish is just as much a Chicana as one who speaks several variants of Spanish. A Chicana from Michigan or Chicago or Detroit is just as much a Chicana as one from the Southwest. Chicano Spanish is as diverse linguistically as it is regionally.

By the end of this century, Spanish speakers will comprise the biggest minority group in the U.S., a country where students in high schools and colleges are encouraged to take French classes because French is considered more "cultured." But for a language to remain alive it must be used.[6] By the end of this century English, and not Spanish, will be the mother tongue of most Chicanos and Latinos.

So, if you want to really hurt me, talk badly about my language. Ethnic identity is twin skin to linguistic identity—I am my language.

---

[6]Irena Klepfisz, "Secular Jewish Identity: Yidishkayt in American," in *The Tribe of Dina,* Kaye/Kantrowitz and Klepfisz, eds., 43.

Until I can take pride in my language, I cannot take pride in myself. Until I can accept as legitimate Chicano Texas Spanish, Tex-Mex and all the other languages I speak, I cannot accept the legitimacy of myself. Until I am free to write bilingually and to switch codes without having always to translate, while I still have to speak English or Spanish when I would rather speak Spanglish, and as long as I have to accommodate the English speakers rather than having them accommodate me, my tongue will be illegitimate.

I will no longer be made to feel ashamed of existing. I will have my voice: Indian, Spanish, white. I will have my serpent's tongue— my woman's voice, my sexual voice, my poet's voice. I will overcome the tradition of silence.

> My fingers
> move sly against your palm
> Like women everywhere, we speak in code. . . .
> —Melanie Kaye/Kantrowitz[7]

"Vistas," corridos, y comida: My Native Tongue

In the 1960s, I read my first Chicano novel. It was *City of Night* by John Rechy, a gay Texan, son of a Scottish father and a Mexican mother. For days I walked around in stunned amazement that a Chicano could write and could get published. When I read *I Am Joaquín*[8] I was surprised to see a bilingual book by a Chicano in print. When I saw poetry written in Tex-Mex for the first time, a feeling of pure joy flashed through me. I felt like we really existed as a people. In 1971, when I started teaching High School English to Chicano students, I tried to supplement required texts with works by Chicanos, only to be reprimanded and forbidden to do so by the principal. He claimed that I was supposed to teach "American" and English literature. At the risk of being fired, I swore my students to secrecy and slipped in Chicano short stories, poems, a play. In graduate school, while working toward a Ph.D., I had to "argue" with one advisor after the other, semester

---

[7]Melanie Kaye/Kantrowitz, "Sign," in *We Speak in Code: Poems and other Writings* (Pittsburgh, PA: Motheroot Publications, Inc., 1980), 85.

[8]Rodolfo Gonzales, *I Am Joaquín/Yo Soy Joaquín* (New York, NY: Bantam Books, 1972). It was first published in 1967.

after semester, before I was allowed to make Chicano literature an area of focus.

Even before I read books by Chicanos or Mexicans, it was the
Mexican movies I saw at the drive-in—the Thursday night specials of $1.00 a carload—that gave me a sense of belonging. "*Vámonos a las vistas,*" my mother would call out and we'd all—grandmother, brothers, sister and cousins—squeeze into the car. We'd wolf down cheese and bologna white bread sandwiches while watching Pedro Infante in melodramatic tearjerkers like *Nosotros los pobres,* the first "real" Mexican movie (that was not an imitation of European movies). I remember seeing *Cuando los hijos se van* and surmising that all Mexican movies played up the love a mother has for her children and what ungrateful sons and daughters suffer when they are not devoted to their mothers. I remember the singing-type "westerns" of Jorge Negrete and Miquel Aceves Mejía. When watching Mexican movies, I felt a sense of homecoming as well as alienation. People who were to amount to something didn't go to Mexican movies, or *bailes* or tune their radios to *bolero, rancherita,* and *corrido* music.

The whole time I was growing up, there was *norteño* music, sometimes called North Mexican border music, or Tex-Mex music, or Chicano music, or *cantina* (bar) music. I grew up listening to *conjuntos,* three- or four-piece bands made up of folk musicians playing guitar, *baja sexto,* drums and button accordion, which Chicanos had borrowed from the German immigrants who had come to Central Texas and Mexico to farm and build breweries. In the Rio Grande Valley, Steve Jordan and Little Joe Hernández were popular, and Flaco Jiménez was the accordion king. The rhythms of Tex-Mex music are those of the polka, also adapted from the Germans, who in turn had borrowed the polka from the Czechs and Bohemians.

I remember the hot, sultry evenings when *corridos*—songs of love and death on the Texas-Mexican borderlands—reverberated out of cheap amplifiers from the local *cantinas* and wafted in through my bedroom window.

Corridos first became widely used along the South Texas/Mexican border during the early conflict between Chicanos and Anglos. The *corridos* are usually about Mexican heroes who do valiant deeds against the Anglo oppressors. Pancho Villa's song, *"La cucaracha,"* is the most famous one. *Corridos* of John F. Kennedy and his death are still very popular in the Valley. Older Chicanos remember Lydia Mendoza, one of the great border corrido singers who was called *la Gloria de Tejas*. Her *"El tango negro,"* sung during the Great Depression, made her a singer of the people. The ever present *corridos* narrated one hundred years of border history, bringing news of events as well as entertaining. These folk musicians and folk songs are our chief cultural mythmakers, and they made our hard lives seem bearable.

I grew up feeling ambivalent about our music. Country-western and rock-and-roll had more status. In the 50s and 60s, for the slightly educated and *agringado* Chicanos, there existed a sense of shame at being caught listening to our music. Yet I couldn't stop my feet from thumping to the music, could not stop humming the words, nor hide from myself the exhilaration I felt when I heard it.

35   There are more subtle ways that we internalize identification, especially in the forms of images and emotions. For me food and certain smells are tied to my identity, to my homeland. Woodsmoke curling up to an immense blue sky; woodsmoke perfuming my grandmother's clothes, her skin. The stench of cow manure and the yellow patches on the ground; the crack of a .22 rifle and the reek of cordite. Homemade white cheese sizzling in a pan, melting inside a folded *tortilla*. My sister Hilda's hot, spicy *menudo, chile colorado* making it deep red, pieces of *panza* and hominy floating on top. My brother Carito barbecuing *fajitas* in the backyard. Even now and 3,000 miles away, I can see my mother spicing the ground beef, pork and venison with *chile*. My mouth salivates at the thought of the hot steaming *tamales* I would be eating if I were home.

Si le preguntas a mi mamá, "¿Qué eres?"

> Identity is the essential core of who
> we are as individuals, the conscious
> experience of the self inside.
>   —Kaufman[9]

Nosotros los chicanos straddle the borderlands. On one side of us, we are constantly exposed to the Spanish of the Mexicans, on the other side we hear the Anglos' incessant clamoring so that we forget our language. Among ourselves we don't say *nosotros los americanos, o nosotros*

---

[9]Kaufman, 68.

los españoles, o nosotros los hispanos. We say *nosotros los mexicanos* (by *mexicanos* we do not mean citizens of Mexico; we do not mean a national identity, but a racial one). We distinguish between *mexicanos del otro lado* and *mexicanos de este lado*. Deep in our hearts we believe that being Mexican has nothing to do with which country one lives in. Being Mexican is a state of soul—not one of mind, not one of citizenship. Neither eagle nor serpent, but both. And like the ocean, neither animal respects borders.

> *Dime con quien andas y te diré quien eres.*
> (Tell me who your friends are and I'll tell you who
> you are.)
>
> —Mexican saying

Si le preguntas a mi mamá, "¿Qué eres?" te dirá. "Soy mexicana." My brothers and sisters say the same. I sometimes will answer *"soy mexicana"* and at others will say *"soy chicana" o "soy tejana."* But I identified as *"Raza"* before I ever identified as *"mexicana"* or *"chicana"*.

As a culture, we call ourselves Spanish when referring to ourselves as a linguistic group and when copping out. It is then that we forget our predominant Indian genes. We are 70–80% Indian.[10] We call ourselves Hispanic[11] or Spanish-American or Latin-American or Latin when linking ourselves to other Spanish-speaking peoples of the Western hemisphere and when copping out. We call ourselves Mexican-American[12] to signify we are neither Mexican nor American, but more the noun "American" than the adjective "Mexican" (and when copping out).

Chicanos and other people of color suffer economically for not acculturating. This voluntary (yet forced) alienation makes for psychological conflict, a kind of dual identity—we don't identify with the Anglo-American cultural values and we don't totally identify with the Mexican cultural values. We are a synergy of the two cultures with various degrees of Mexicanness or Angloness. I have so internalized the borderland conflict that sometimes I feel like one cancels out the

---

[10]Hernández-Chávez, 88–90.

[11]"Hispanic" is derived from *Hispania (España),* a name given to the Iberian Peninsula in ancient times when it was part of the Roman Empire, and is a term designated by the U.S. government to make it easier to handle us on paper.

[12]The Treaty of Guadalupe Hidalgo created the Mexican-American in 1848.

other and we are zero, nothing, no one. *A veces no soy nada ni nadie. Pero hasta cuando no lo soy, lo soy.*

40   When not copping out, when we know we are more than noth-   40
ing, we call ourselves Mexican, referring to race and ancestry; *mestizo*
when affirming both our Indian and Spanish (but we hardly ever own
our Black ancestry); Chicano when referring to a politically aware people born and/or raised in the U.S.; *Raza* when referring to Chicanos;
tejanos when we are Chicanos from Texas.

Chicanos did not know we were a people until 1965 when César
Chávez and the farmworkers united and *I Am Joaquín* was published
and *la Raza Unida* party was formed in Texas. With that recognition,
we became a distinct people. Something momentous happened to the
Chicano soul—we became aware of our reality and acquired a name
and a language (Chicano Spanish) that reflected that reality. Now that
we had a name, some of the fragmented pieces began to fall
together—who we were, what we were, how we had evolved. We
began to get glimpses of what we might eventually become.

Yet the struggle of identities continues, the struggle of borders is
our reality still. One day the inner struggle will cease and a true inte-
gration take place. In the meantime, *tenemos que hacer la lucha. ¿Quién
está protegiendo los ranchos de mi gente? ¿Quién está tratando de cerrar
la fisura entre la india y el blanco en nuestra sangre? El chicano, si, el chicano que anda como un ladrón en su propia casa.*

Los chicanos, how patient we seem, how very patient. There is the
quiet of the Indian about us.[13] We know how to survive. When other
races have given up their tongue, we've kept ours. We know what it is
to live under the hammer blow of the dominant *norteamericano* culture. But more than we count the blows, we count the days the weeks
the years the centuries the eons until the white laws and commerce
and customs will rot in the deserts they've created, lie bleached. *Hu-
mildes* yet proud, *quietos* yet wild, *nosotros los mexicanos-chicanos* will
walk by the crumbling ashes as we go about our business. Stubborn,
persevering, impenetrable as stone, yet possessing a malleability that
renders us unbreakable, we, the *mestizas* and *mestizos,* will remain.

---

[13]Anglos, in order to alleviate their guilt for dispossessing the Chicano, stressed the Spanish part of us and perpetuated the myth of the Spanish Southwest. We have accepted
the fiction that we are Hispanic, that is Spanish, in order to accommodate ourselves to
the dominant culture and its abhorrence of Indians. Hernández-Chávez, 88–91.

Questions on Meaning

1. To Anzaldúa, language—and one's feeling about one's language—plays a large role in one's self-image. How do Chicanos use their language to oppress each other? What must Chicanos do to keep their language alive?
2. Why does Anzaldúa say that "Chicano Spanish is not incorrect; it is a living language"? What aspects of Chicanos' lives influenced its present form?
3. What was Anzaldúa's reaction when she read her first Chicano novel? Why did she react so strongly? What happened when she attempted to introduce Chicano literature to others?

Questions on Rhetorical Strategy and Style

1. Anzaldúa blends standard English with many variants of Spanish in her essay. What was your initial reaction to this writing style? Explain how your reaction changed as you read the essay, notably after her comments about writing bilingually. What language *form* do you feel her writing style exemplifies? If you cannot read Spanish, what do you feel you might have missed by being unable to read her Spanish comments?
2. Find the many examples Anzaldúa provides to illustrate the development of the Spanish spoken by Chicanos. Locate other passages where she uses examples.
3. How does Anzaldúa define "*poshismos*," "*pocho*," and "*Pachuco*"? Why does she say that she has lost most of her *Pachuco*? How does Anzaldúa's experience with *Pachuco* reinforce her contention about the importance of language to an individual's identity?

Writing Assignments

1. Anzaldúa states that "by *mexicanos* we do not mean a national identity." What other ethnic groups in America today might make a similar statement? What does this statement say about Chicanos' self-image?
2. Anzaldúa notes that the practice of describing an individual by a word form that uses the individual's ancestry as an adjective and "American" as a noun—as in Mexican-American—places emphasis on "American" at the expense of their ethnic background. Do

you agree? Explain why you think we should or should not reverse the form of these words to American-Mexican, American-African, American-Chinese, etc.

3. Research Cesar Chavez and his work with farm workers. Write an essay on the impact of Chavez's work. What were his tactics? Did he achieve all he set out to achieve? What individuals and groups opposed his initiatives? How did his work with migrant farm-workers, who were largely American-Mexicans, affect working conditions of other workers? What is his legacy?

⌒ WE REAL COOL ⌒

Gwendolyn Brooks

Gwendolyn Brooks (1917-) was born in Topeka, Kansas, but has lived her life in Chicago and has become one of the most beloved of Illinois poets. She attended Wilson Junior College in Chicago and was graduated in 1938. Her first poem, "Eventide," appeared in the magazine American Childhood *when she was yet in her early teens. She published many poems in the* Chicago Defender, *a local paper. Her first book of poems,* A Street in Bronzeville *was published in 1945.* Annie Allen *(1949) won Brooks a Pulitzer Prize. Other collections of her poetry include* Bronzeville Boy and Girls *(1956),* The Bean Eaters *(1960),* Selected Poems *(1963),* In the Mecca *(1968),* Riot *(1969),* Blacks *(1987), and* Children Coming Home *(1991). She also has written an autobiographical novel,* Maud Martha *(1953) and a book of memoirs,* Report from Part One *(1972). "We Real Cool" expresses the quality of life in the city for young African-American men in the early 1960s.*

The Pool Players.
Seven at the Golden Shovel.

We real cool. We
Left school. We

Lurk late. We
Strike straight. We

Sing sin. We
Thin gin. We

Jazz June. We
Die soon.

Questions on Meaning

1. The subtitle of "We Real Cool" is "The Pool Players. Seven at the Golden Shovel." What associations does the poem make with pool playing and the life of young men?
2. Does Brooks' poem have a political edge? What persuasive intention might she have for the speakers in the poem and for her readers?
3. The speakers in "We Real Cool" may become an example to other young people. Does Brooks seem to be giving a reason for picking these particular young men for her example of the dangerous life? Why?

Questions on Rhetorical Strategy and Style

1. What kind of language is Brooks approximating in the poem? What kinds of reactions might readers have to that language?
2. Who is speaking in the poem, and what is the reader supposed to think and feel about the speakers?
3. The life of the youngsters in the poem will clearly lead to a bad end, or so says the poem. What chain of causation does the poem imply? Do young people believe that their actions will lead to bad effects?

Writing Assignments

1. Find current rap lyrics that use the same types of rhythm and style as Brooks' poem. Write about your reaction to the effects of these rhythms.
2. Does the social commentary in the poem have as strong an effect in the beginning of the twenty-first century as it did in the middle of the twentieth century? What does your answer to this question say about human progress?
3. "We Real Cool" appears to be about not growing up, but what does it say about the need to grow up? Write an essay or poem that give examples of behaviors that imply acceptance of adult responsibilities.

❧ MAMMAS DON'T LET ❧
YOUR BABIES GROW UP
TO BE COWBOYS

Ed Bruce and Patsy Bruce

(As Adapted and Performed by Willie Nelson with Waylon Jennings) (1975)

Mammas don't let your babies grow up to be cowboys
Don't let 'em pick guitars and drive them old trucks
Make 'em be doctors and lawyers and such
Mammas don't let your babies grow up to be cowboys
They'll never stay home and they're always alone
Even with someone they love

Cowboys ain't easy to love and they're hard to hold
And they'd rather give you a song than diamonds or gold
Lonestar belt buckles and old faded Levi's
Each night begins a new day
And if you don't understand him he won't die young
He'll probably just ride away.

Mammas don't let your babies grow up to be cowboys
Don't let 'em pick guitars and drive them old trucks
Make 'em be doctors and lawyers and such
Mammas don't let your babies grow up to be cowboys
They'll never stay home and they're always alone
Even with someone they love.

Cowboys like smoky old pool rooms and cool mountain mornings
Little warm puppies and children and girls of the night
And them that don't know him won't like him
And them that do sometimes won't know how to take him
He ain't wrong, he's just different
But his pride won't let him do things to make you think he's right.

Mammas don't let your babies grow up to be cowboys
Don't let 'em pick guitars and drive them old trucks
Make 'em be doctors and lawyers and such
Mammas don't let your babies grow up to be cowboys
They'll never stay home and they're always alone
Even with someone they love.

"Hollywood and many history writers are mighty guilty of misrepresenting the story. I got pretty angry when I began to read about black cowboys. One out of every three or four cowboys was either black or Mexican. We've been fed this image of the white cowboy, and I'm out to retake some visual territory with these paintings. My cowboys are symbols of the untold and whitewashed history of colored people who are part of the American story."

—Bernard Williams

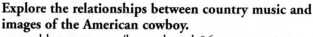

Explore the relationships between country music and images of the American cowboy.
www.ablongman.com/beyondwords06

Consider

1. What do you think the songwriters mean when they advise mothers against raising their children to be cowboys? What do these lyrics suggest about the rewards and drawbacks of cowboy life? Do you think the advice in the song is serious? Why or why not?

2. Analyze the composition and design elements used in the painting *Sergeant Buffalo*. What can you say about how Williams uses his medium to convey a political and historical argument? Do you think the painting is effective in conveying that argument? Explain.

Compose

3. In the library or on the Internet, research how cowboys have been portrayed in the popular media during the past fifty years. Write a short essay describing the patterns you see, incorporating specific images and examples that illustrate those patterns.

4. Imagine that you've been commissioned to create a portrait that accurately documents and preserves for future generations a group that you belong to. What medium would you choose? What would the portrait include? Write a paragraph describing the portrait you would create (or actually create the portrait).

☞ LIVING WITH MUSIC ☜

Ralph Ellison

Ralph Ellison (1919–1994) studied music and literature at the Tuskegee Institute. He lacked the money to finish college, but he did not lack the talent to write, in 1952, one of the classic novels of modern American literature, Invisible Man. *Ellison taught at New York University and lectured at many other universities. Ellison writes in the complex and subtle style favored by academic intellectuals; his style made the black experience uniquely available to an educated white audience.*

In those days it was either live with music or die with noise, and we chose rather desperately to live. In the process our apartment—what with its booby-trappings of audio equipment, wires, discs and tapes—came to resemble the Collier mansion, but that was later. First there was the neighborhood, assorted drunks and a singer.

We were living at the time in a tiny ground-floor-rear apartment in which I was also trying to write. I say "trying" advisedly. To our right, separated by a thin wall, was a small restaurant with a juke box the size of the Roxy. To our left, a night-employed swing enthusiast who took his lullaby music so loud that every morning promptly at nine Basie's brasses started blasting my typewriter off its stand. Our living room looked out across a small back yard to a rough stone wall to an apartment building which, towering above, caught every passing thoroughfare sound and rifled it straight down to me. There were also howling cats and barking dogs, none capable of music worth living with, so we'll pass them by.

But the court behind the wall, which on the far side came knee-high to a short Iroquois, was a forum for various singing and/or preaching drunks who wandered back from the corner bar. From these you sometimes heard a fair barbershop style "Bill Bailey," free-wheeling versions of "The Bastard King of England," the saga of Uncle Bud, or a deeply felt rendition of Leroy Carr's "How Long Blues." The preaching drunks took on any topic that came to mind: current events, the fate of the long-sunk *Titanic* or the relative merits of the Giants and the Dodgers. Naturally there was great argument and occasional fighting—none of it fatal but all of it loud.

I shouldn't complain, however, for these were rather entertaining drunks, who like the birds appeared in the spring and left with the first fall cold. A more dedicated fellow was there all the time, day and night, come rain, come shine. Up on the corner lived a drunk of legend, a true phenomenon, who could surely have qualified as the king of all the world's winos—not excluding the French. He was neither poetic like the others nor ambitious like the singer (to whom we'll presently come) but his drinking bouts were truly awe-inspiring and he was not without his sensitivity. In the throes of his passion he would shout to the whole wide world one concise command, "Shut up!" Which was disconcerting enough to all who heard (except, perhaps, the singer), but such were the labyrinthine acoustics of courtyards and areaways that he seemed to direct his command at me. The writer's block which this produced is indescribable. On one heroic occasion he yelled his obsessive command without one interruption longer than necessary to take another drink (and with no appreciable loss of volume, penetration or authority) for three long summer days and nights, and shortly afterwards he died. Just how many lines of agitated prose he cost me I'll never know, but in all that chaos of sound I sympathized with his obsession, for I, too, hungered and thirsted for quiet. Nor did he inspire me to a painful identification, and for that I was thankful. Identification, after all, involves feelings of guilt and responsibility, and since I could hardly hear my own typewriter keys I felt in no way accountable for his condition. We were simply fellow victims of the madding crowd. May he rest in peace.

5   No, these more involved feelings were aroused by a more intimate   5
source of noise, one that got beneath the skin and worked into the very structure of one's consciousness—like the "fate" motif in Beethoven's Fifth or the knocking-at-the-gates scene in *Macbeth*. For at the top of our pyramid of noise there was a singer who lived directly above us, you might say we had a singer on our ceiling.

Now, I had learned from the jazz musicians I had known as a boy in Oklahoma City something of the discipline and devotion to his art required of the artist. Hence I knew something of what the singer faced. These jazzmen, many of them now world-famous, lived for and with music intensely. Their driving motivation was neither money nor fame, but the will to achieve the most eloquent expression of idea-emotions through the technical mastery of their instruments (which, incidentally, some of them wore as a priest wears the cross) and the give and take, the subtle rhythmical shaping and blending of idea, tone and imagination demanded of group improvisation. The delicate balance struck between strong individual personality and the group during those early jam sessions was a marvel of social organization. I had learned too that the end of all this discipline and technical mastery was the desire to express an affirmative way of life through its musical tradition and that this tradition insisted that each artist achieve his creativity within its frame. He must learn the best of the past, and add to it his personal vision. Life could be harsh, loud and wrong if it wished, but they lived it fully, and when they expressed their attitude toward the world it was with a fluid style that reduced the chaos of living to form.

The objectives of these jazzmen were not at all those of the singer on our ceiling, but though a purist committed to the mastery of the *bel canto* style, German *lieder*, modern French art songs and a few American slave songs sung as if *bel canto*, she was intensely devoted to her art. From morning to night she vocalized, regardless of the condition of her voice, the weather or my screaming nerves. There were times when her notes, sifting through her floor and my ceiling, bouncing down the walls and ricocheting off the building in the rear, whistled like ten-penny nails, buzzed like a saw, wheezed like the asthma of a Hercules, trumpeted like an enraged African elephant—and the squeaky pedal of her piano rested plumb center above my typing chair. After a year of non-co-operation from the neighbor on my left I became desperate enough to cool down the hot blast of his phonograph by calling the cops, but the singer presented a serious ethical problem: Could I, an aspiring artist, complain against the hard work and devotion to craft of another aspiring artist?

Then there was my sense of guilt. Each time I prepared to shatter the ceiling in protest I was restrained by the knowledge that I, too, during my boyhood, had tried to master a musical instrument and to the great distress of my neighbors—perhaps even greater than that which I now suffered. For while our singer was concerned basically with a single tradition and style, I had been caught actively between two: that of the Negro folk music, both sacred and profane, slave song and jazz, and that of Western classical music. It was most confusing; the folk tradition demanded that I play what I heard and felt around me, while those who were seeking to teach the classical tradition in the schools insisted that I play strictly according to the book and express that which I was *supposed* to feel. This sometimes led to heated clashes of wills. Once during a third-grade music appreciation class a friend of mine insisted that it was a large green snake he saw swimming down a quiet brook instead of the snowy bird the teacher felt that Saint-Saëns' *Carnival of the Animals* should evoke. The rest of us sat there and lied like little black, brown and yellow Trojans about that swan, but our stalwart classmate held firm to his snake. In the end he got himself spanked and reduced the teacher to tears, but truth, reality and our environment were redeemed. For we were all familiar with snakes, while a swan was simply something the Ugly Duckling of the story grew up to be. Fortunately some of us grew up with a genuine appreciation of classical music despite such teaching methods. But as an aspiring trumpeter I was to wallow in sin for years before being awakened to guilt by our singer.

Caught mid-range between my two traditions, where one attitude often clashed with the other and one technique of playing was by the other opposed, I caused whole blocks of people to suffer.

10   Indeed, I terrorized a good part of an entire city section. During   10
summer vacation I blew sustained tones out of the window for hours, usually starting—especially on Sunday mornings—before breakfast. I sputtered whole days through M. Arban's (he's the great authority on the instrument) double- and triple-tonguing exercises with an effect like that of a jackass hiccupping off a big meal of briars. During school-term mornings I practiced a truly exhibitionist "Reveille" before leaving for school, and in the evening I generously gave the ever-listening world a long, slow version of "Taps," ineptly played but throbbing with what I in my adolescent vagueness felt was a romantic sadness. For it was farewell to day and a love song to life and a peace-be-with-you to all the dead and dying.

On hot summer afternoons I tormented the ears of all not blessedly deaf with imitations of the latest hot solos of Hot Lips Paige (then a local hero), the leaping right hand of Earl "Fatha" Hines, or the rowdy poetic flights of Louis Armstrong. Naturally I rehearsed also such school-band standbys as the *Light Cavalry Overture*, Sousa's *"Stars and Stripes Forever,"* the *William Tell Overture,* and *"Tiger Rag."*

(Not even an after-school job as office boy to a dentist could stop my efforts. Frequently, by way of encouraging my development in the proper cultural direction, the dentist asked me proudly to render Schubert's *Serenade* for some poor devil with his jaw propped open in the dental chair. When the drill got going, or the forceps bit deep, I blew real strong.)

Sometimes, inspired by the even then considerable virtuosity of the late Charlie Christian (who during our school days played marvelous riffs on a cigar box banjo), I'd give whole summer afternoons and the evening hours after heavy suppers of black-eyed peas and turnip greens, cracklin' bread and buttermilk, lemonade and sweet potato cobbler, to practicing hard-driving blues. Such food oversupplied me with bursting energy, and from listening to Ma Rainey, Ida Cox and Clara Smith, who made regular appearances in our town, I knew exactly how I wanted my horn to sound. But in the effort to make it do so (I was no embryo Joe Smith or Tricky Sam Nanton) I sustained the curses of both Christian and infidel—along with the encouragement of those more sympathetic citizens who understood the profound satisfaction to be found in expressing oneself in the blues.

Despite those who complained and cried to heaven for Gabriel to blow a chorus so heavenly sweet and so hellishly hot that I'd forever put down my horn, there were more tolerant ones who were willing to pay in present pain for future pride.

For who knew what skinny kid with his chops wrapped around a trumpet mouthpiece and a faraway look in his eyes might become the next Armstrong? Yes, and send you, at some big dance a few years hence, into an ecstasy of rhythm and memory and brassy affirmation of the goodness of being alive and part of the community? Someone had to; for it was part of the group tradition—though that was not how they said it.

"Let that boy blow," they'd say to the protesting ones. "He's got to talk baby talk on that thing before he can preach on it. Next thing you know he's liable to be up there with Duke Ellington. Sure, plenty Oklahoma boys are up there with the big bands. Son, let's hear you try those 'Trouble in Mind Blues.' Now try and make it sound like ole Ida Cox sings it."

And I'd draw in my breath and do Miss Cox great violence.

Thus the crimes and aspirations of my youth. It had been years since I had played the trumpet or irritated a single ear with other than the spoken or written word, but as far as my singing neighbor was concerned I had to hold my peace. I was forced to listen, and in listening I soon became involved to the point of identification. If she sang badly I'd hear my own futility in the windy sound; if well, I'd stare at my typewriter and despair that I should ever make my prose so sing. She left me neither night nor day, this singer on our ceiling, and as my writing languished I became more and more upset. Thus one desperate morning I decided that since I seemed doomed to live within a shrieking chaos I might as well contribute my share; perhaps if I fought noise with noise I'd attain some small peace. Then a miracle: I turned on my radio (an old Philco AM set connected to a small Pilot FM tuner) and I heard the words

Art thou troubled?
Music will calm thee . . .

I stopped as though struck by the voice of an angel. It was Kathleen Ferrier, that loveliest of singers, giving voice to the aria from Handel's *Rodelinda.* The voice was so completely expressive of words and music that I accepted it without question—what lover of the vocal art could resist her?

Yet it was ironic, for after giving up my trumpet for the typewriter I had avoided too close a contact with the very art which she recommended as balm. For I had started music early and lived with it daily, and when I broke I tried to break clean. Now in this magical moment all the old love, the old fascination with music superbly rendered, flooded back. When she finished I realized that with such music in my own apartment, the chaotic sounds from without and above had sunk, if not into silence, then well below the level where they mattered. Here was a way out. If I was to live and write in that apartment, it would be only through the grace of music. I had tuned in a Ferrier recital, and when it ended I rushed out for several of her records, certain that now deliverance was mine.

But not yet. Between the hi-fi record and the ear, I learned, there was a new electronic world. In that realization our apartment was well on its way toward becoming an audio booby trap. It was 1949 and I rushed to the Audio Fair. I have, I confess, as much gadget-resistance as the next American of my age, weight and slight income; but little did I dream of the test to which it would be put. I had hardly entered the fair before I heard David Sarser's and Mel Sprinkle's Musician's

Amplifier, took a look at its schematic and, recalling a boyhood acquaintance with such matters, decided that I could build one. I did, several times before it measured within specifications. And still our system was lacking. Fortunately my wife shared my passion for music, so we went on to buy, piece by piece, a fine speaker system, a first-rate AM-FM tuner, a transcription turntable and a speaker cabinet. I built half a dozen or more preamplifiers and record compensators before finding a commercial one that satisfied my ear, and, finally, we acquired an arm, a magnetic cartridge and—glory of the house—a tape recorder. All this plunge into electronics, mind you, had as its simple end the enjoyment of recorded music as it was intended to be heard. I was obsessed with the idea of reproducing sound with such fidelity that even when using music as a defense behind which I could write, it would reach the unconscious levels of the mind with the least distortion. And it didn't come easily. There were wires and pieces of equipment all over the tiny apartment (I became a compulsive experimenter) and it was worth your life to move about without first taking careful bearings. Once we were almost crushed in our sleep by the tape machine, for which there was space only on a shelf at the head of our bed. But it was worth it.

20   For now when we played a recording on our system even the 20 drunks on the wall could recognize its quality. I'm ashamed to admit, however, that I did not always restrict its use to the demands of pleasure or defense. Indeed, with such marvels of science at my control I lost my humility. My ethical consideration for the singer up above shriveled like a plant in too much sunlight. For instead of soothing, music seemed to release the beast in me. Now when jarred from my writer's reveries by some especially enthusiastic flourish of our singer, I'd rush to my music system with blood in my eyes and burst a few decibels in her direction. If she defied me with a few more pounds of pressure against her diaphragm, then a war of decibels was declared.

If, let us say, she were singing *"Depuis le Jour"* from *Louise,* I'd put on a tape of Bidu Sayão performing the same aria, and let the rafters ring. If it was some song by Mahler, I'd match her spitefully with Marian Anderson or Kathleen Ferrier; if she offended with something from *Der Rosenkavalier,* I'd attack her flank with Lotte Lehmann. If she brought me up from my desk with art songs by Ravel or Rachmaninoff, I'd defend myself with Maggie Teyte or Jennie Tourel. If she polished a spiritual to a meaningless artiness I'd play Bessie Smith to remind her of the earth out of which we came. Once in a while I'd forget completely that I was supposed to be a gentleman and blast her with Strauss' *Zarathustra,* Bartók's *Concerto for Orchestra,* Ellington's "Flaming Sword," the famous crescendo from *The Pines of Rome,* or Satchmo scatting, "I'll be Glad When You're Dead" (you rascal you!). Oh, I was living with music with a sweet vengeance.

One might think that all this would have made me her most hated enemy, but not at all. When I met her on the stoop a few weeks after my rebellion, expecting her fully to slap my face, she astonished me by complimenting our music system. She even questioned me concerning the artists I had used against her. After that, on days when the acoustics were right, she'd stop singing until the piece was finished and then applaud—not always, I guessed, without a justifiable touch of sarcasm. And although I was now getting on with my writing, the unfairness of this business bore in upon me. Aware that I could not have withstood a similar comparison with literary artists of like caliber, I grew remorseful. I also came to admire the singer's courage and control, for she was neither intimidated into silence nor goaded into undisciplined screaming; she persevered, she marked the phrasing of the great singers I sent her way, she improved her style.

Better still, she vocalized more softly, and I, in turn, used music less and less as a weapon and more for its magic with mood and memory. After a while a simple twirl of the volume control up a few decibels and down again would bring a live-and-let-live reduction of her volume. We have long since moved from that apartment and that most interesting neighborhood and now the floors and walls of our present apartment are adequately thick and there is even a closet large enough to house the audio system; the only wire visible is that leading from the closet to the corner speaker system. Still we are indebted to the singer and the old environment for forcing us to discover one of the most deeply satisfying aspects of our living. Perhaps the enjoyment of music is always suffused with past experience; for me, at least, this is true.

It seems a long way and a long time from the glorious days of Oklahoma jazz dances, the jam sessions at Halley Richardson's place on Deep Second, from the phonographs shouting the blues in the back alleys I knew as a delivery boy and from the days when watermelon men with voices like mellow bugles shouted their wares in time with the rhythm of their horses' hoofs and farther still from the washerwomen singing slave songs as they stirred sooty tubs in sunny yards, and a long time, too, from those intense, conflicting days when the school music program of Oklahoma City was tuning our earthy young ears to classical accents—with music appreciation classes and free musical instruments and basic instruction for any child who cared to learn and uniforms for all who made the band. There was a mistaken notion on the part of some of the teachers that classical music had nothing to do with the rhythms, relaxed or hectic, of daily living, and that one should crook the little finger when listening to such refined strains. And the blues and the spirituals—jazz—? they would have destroyed them and scattered the pieces. Nevertheless, we learned some of it all, for in the United States when traditions are juxtaposed they tend, regardless of what we do to prevent it, irresistibly to merge. Thus musically at least each child in our town was an heir of all the ages. One learns by moving from the familiar to the unfamiliar, and while it might sound incongruous at first, the step from the spirituality of the spirituals to that of the Beethoven of the symphonies or the Bach of the chorales is not as vast as it seems. Nor is the romanticism of a Brahms or Chopin completely unrelated to that of Louis Armstrong. Those who know their native culture and love it unchauvinistically are never lost when encountering the unfamiliar.

25   Living with music today we find Mozart and Ellington, Kirsten   25
Flagstad and Chippie Hill, William L. Dawson and Carl Orff all forming part of our regular fare. For all exalt life in rhythm and melody; all add to its significance. Perhaps in the swift change of American society in which the meanings of one's origin are so quickly lost, one of the chief values of living with music lies in its power to give us an orientation in time. In doing so, it gives significance to all those indefinable aspects of experience which nevertheless help to make us what we are. In the swift whirl of time music is a constant, reminding us of what we were and of that toward which we aspired. Art thou troubled? Music will not only calm, it will ennoble thee.

Questions on Meaning

1. Many of Ellison's references—for example "the Collier mansion," "Basie's brasses," and "knee high to a short Iroquois"—rely on specialized knowledge. Find a few references that seem mysterious to you and make your best guess at explaining what they are supposed to mean in the context.
2. The essay opens with the thesis that "it was either live with music or die with noise." List the main points by which Ellison develops this idea.

Questions on Rhetorical Strategy and Style

1. Ellison describes a drunk in elaborately formal terms (such as "in the throes of his passion he would shout to the whole wide world one concise command, 'Shut up!'"). What effect does he intend with this formal language?
2. Why does Ellison go to such great lengths to assemble equipment to play music in his apartment?
3. The point of the essay turns on a pair of definitions—of *music* and *noise*—that Ellison develops implicitly throughout the essay. Define these two key terms in the context of Ellison's essay.

Writing Assignments

1. Write an essay about a conflict you've had with neighbors over noise or some other issue.
2. Read some music or stereo equipment reviews (e.g., in *Rolling Stone* or *Audiophile*) and write your own review of a recent CD or piece of equipment.

DEBATING CULTURE:
WRITING TO ADVOCATE
AND PERSUADE

YOU CAN CLICK
BUT YOU
CAN'T HIDE

| I | ILLEGAL DOWNLOADING
| | Inappropriate for All Ages |

If you think you can get away with illegally swapping movies, you're wrong. Illegally trafficking in movies is not just a dirty little secret between you and your computer. You leave a trail. The message is simple: if you are downloading copyrighted movies without proper authorization, you are breaking the law. You face serious consequences if you illegally swap movies. The only way not to get caught is to stop.

Pursuant to the Copyright Act (17 U.S.C. Section 504(c)), statutory damages can be as much as $30,000 per motion picture, and up to $150,000 per motion picture if the infringement is willful.

KEEPING ITS COOL: MTV STAYS HIP—AND POWERFUL—BY REMAINING INDISPENSABLE TO MUSIC, FASHION, AND MOVIES

Patrick Goldstein

The people on MTV may come and go with the rapidity for which the MTV style is famous, but the company itself has been around successfully for over 20 years and is still going strong. What makes MTV forever hip when one quality of hip is to disdain the style that was deemed hip only a minute ago? Journalist Patrick Goldstein investigates the MTV phenomenon with interviews and analysis. Perhaps his examples may seem dated, but how about the conclusions he makes that predict that dating?

Waiting in line at the post office the other day, I had time to peruse a giant poster advertising a new stamp featuring the dewy visage of James Dean. He'd be 70 if he were still alive, but on his stamp, he's as beguiling as always. You can be hip forever if you never grow old, which is why Dean and Jim Morrison and Kurt Cobain are as cool today as the day they died. If you outlive your first burst of success, your cool fades like a vacation tan.

In today's supercharged media culture, hipness is more fleeting than ever. One of the rare exceptions to the rule is MTV, and most of the credit goes to its 55-year-old geezer guru Tom Freston, the longtime chairman of MTV Networks, who has managed to keep a

Reprinted from *Los Angeles Times,* August 21, 2001.

corporate behemoth light on its feet. Staying cool is hard-wired into the DNA of MTV, which is now a global beacon of American youth culture, shown in 342 million households in 140 countries around the world. The Viacom-owned network (which includes MTV Films as part of its operation) recently celebrated its 20th anniversary, an occasion marked by a flurry of media coverage of MTV's role in influencing pop iconography—Freston even found himself on "Hardball," being interrogated rat-a-tat style by Chris Matthews about MTV's obsession with bare-midriff teen sexuality.

MTV deserves the attention. Love it or hate it—and can I just say right here that "Say What? Karaoke" could be the hokiest show on TV—over the past 20 years, from Madonna to Eminem, MTV has become the ultimate arbiter of teen cool.

MTV had its worst ratings slump in the mid-'90s, when it was slow to drop grunge rock in favor of the teen pop phenomenon. Freston learned his lesson. In youth culture, a new generation arrives roughly every four years. "The tendency in the entertainment business is to take a good thing and milk it dry," Freston says. "But when you're successful is when you should start looking for something new. It would be terrible if people said, 'Geez, MTV is still flogging that 'Unplugged' show. We could change everything at MTV every three or four years, and it would all be for the good.'"

If you're growing up in America, nothing else is remotely as influential as MTV in shaping your taste in music, movies and fashion, the three subjects that absorb roughly 99% of the average teenager's day-to-day brain transmissions. The network's secret of success? It constantly reinvents itself. As MTV Group President Judy McGrath put it recently: "One of our key decisions was to be the forever-young channel, not to stick with Rod Stewart, but constantly embrace whatever was coming down the pike." (When you get old, you simply migrate to VH1 and then TV Land, while your kids watch Nickelodeon, all part of the cradle-to-the-grave umbrella that generated more than $3 billion in revenues for MTV Networks last year.)

"It's hard to be big and be cool too, but when it comes to institutions, MTV is about as corporately cool as you can get," says ex-Virgin Records chief Jeff Ayeroff, who masterminded last year's "Beatles 1" marketing blitzkrieg. "If MTV was just about the bottom line, it would've failed. Tom's brilliance is that whenever things feel complacent, he shakes it up. He knows that if they keep their cool, the money will follow."

MTV has a knack for catching a wave and abandoning it before it hits the beach. When the appeal of all-videos-all-the-time began to wane in the late 1 980s, the network began creating its own new programming. When Hollywood began courting young moviegoers each summer, MTV made itself an indispensable launching pad to promote its films.

It also embraced the disposable nature of our fickle culture long before today's one-hit pop wonders took over the pop charts. Forget about Joe DiMaggio—where have you gone Martha Quinn, Julie Brown, Pauly Shore, Jenny McCarthy and Jesse Camp? MTV is the first network with an attention span as short as its viewers'. "For us, a long-term contract for our personalities is one year," says Freston, who seemed unruffled by the news that "Jackass" star Johnny Knoxville might jump ship after only one season on the high-rated stunt-filled reality show.

"People start with us and then move on. It just gets faster. Mike Judge did 'Beavis and Butt-head' for three or four years. Johnny was on for three weeks, and he was already getting movie offers."

MTV rarely bothers to lock up its talent because it knows each new generation wants its own heroes. "Total Request Live" host Carson Daly will soon be moonlighting as host of NBC's late-night show "Later." Can "Hollywood Squares" be far behind?

The ace MTV has up its sleeve is this: It has a stranglehold on its core audience. If you want to see music videos, you basically have to go to MTV. As Artemis Records chief Danny Goldberg puts it: "One year it's Nirvana, next it's Puffy Combs or Korn or Staind, but if you want to see them, where else are you going to go? The music still frames MTV's identity, which gives them a core audience that's by definition young and hip."

MTV is not afraid to flex its muscles. For years it shut out potential video network rivals by arranging exclusives on major new videos. This summer the network did promotional specials for 20 youth-oriented movies, but studio marketers complain that its willingness to air the specials is closely tied to studios' willingness to buy healthy chunks of advertising on the network. And as *The Times* reported Friday, artists appearing on MTV's annual "Video Music Awards," airing Sept. 6, have to agree not to perform on a wide range of entertainment TV outlets for 30 days preceding the awards, prompting claims by competitors of unfair booking rules.

MTV is more nimble—and thus more hip—than its corporate rivals because it operates from the bottom up, not the top down. Its programming is cheaply produced, so it's more willing to take a risk on an oddball idea than a movie studio that spends $100 million to make and market a film. Ted Demme, now a successful film director, came up with the idea for "Yo! MTV Raps" when he was an intern at the network. Tom Green was discovered doing a local-access TV show—in Canada. One of its shows in development for next year is a real-life sitcom starring Ozzy Osbourne and his family.

"We don't have a Kremlin-like control command where decisions are made at the top," Freston says. "At my age, I certainly don't come in with any great ideas. We have a great young staff who are encouraged to take creative risks. You can't have a lot of second-guessers—that's why 'The Sopranos' is on HBO and not on ABC."

Like the major studios, MTV uses reams of research to stay in touch with its audience. But studios essentially use research to satisfy their audience's lowest-common-denominator reaction to a film. MTV uses research to discover what new pop culture trends are being embraced by its audience's most progressive fringe—the kids known as early adopters.

"What the studios do, and it amazes me, is they make a movie, test it and then they adapt the film to the research, by changing the ending or cutting out an unpopular scene," says Freston. "You can imagine how that makes the creator of the film feel, who's saying, 'So you want to make all these changes because some guy you found on the mall who might be on acid didn't like my movie?' We do research to help our creative people make connections with the leading edge of the culture. The idea is to talk to an extreme skateboarder or a Japanese reggae freak and see if we can catch a change in the wind."

MTV has plenty of stiff challenges ahead. Its critics say it has over-dosed on teen fluff and soap opera programming, making it increasingly difficult for Freston to propagate the advertiser-friendly myth that the network's core audience is 17- to 25-year-olds—judging from the kids in my neighborhood, 15 seems more like it. And if the advertising climate remains sluggish, it will be hard to satisfy Viacom's insistence on achieving a cash-flow growth of 20% a year, as MTV has for the past 14 years.

If anyone can keep MTV on the cutting edge, it will be Freston. When most of today's show-biz tycoons were in their 20s, they were busy climbing the corporate ladder. When Freston was that age, he wandered the globe, emulating his Beat hero Jack Kerouac, ending up spending eight years running a textile company in India. His travels gave the onetime vagabond a restless thirst for exploring new horizons.

"I like having people at MTV who are passionate about pop culture and who like to devour new things, whether it's seeing movies or traveling around the world," he says. "I'm very paranoid of us not being different enough. When people become adults they often become resistant to change. So I'm always looking for people who don't just like new ideas, but who live on them."

Themes, Issues, and Ideas

1. According to Goldstein, why is MTV an exception to the rule in the length of its continued popularity?

2. What does the essay show MTV's management doing about maintaining its exceptional status?

3. According to Goldstein, how does MTV differ from movie studios in their efforts to reshape their products to fit their audiences?

Writing Strategies and Techniques

1. The essay begins with images of James Dean, Jim Morrison, and Kurt Cobain. In your own words, explain how they serve as symbols for a major point about popularity that the essay tries to make.

2. Goldstein moves between his own remarks and quotations from others. Do you find that he makes his transitions between these points of view gracefully and successfully? Explain your answer by analyzing examples.

Suggestions for Writing

1. Goldstein says that "in today's supercharged media culture hipness is more fleeting than ever." Do you find Goldstein still hip himselM Is he fully aware of what is happening now in popular music? Write an essay in which you explain and defend your view.

2. Do you think MTV is still hip? Write and essay in which you explain and defend your view.

Credit

FROM THE MARGINS TO MAINSTREAM: THE POLITICAL POWER OF HIP-HOP

Katina R. Stapleton

Katina R. Stapleton was born in Baltimore, Maryland in 1973. She was graduated in 1995 from the University of Maryland at College Park with a BA in print journalism and entered Duke University's political science department, where she is currently working on a dissertation that examines the role of the media in the urban education policy process. She writes and teaches on the politics of music. In this 1998 article, she describes the musical phenomenon called hip-hop in relation to African-American and youth culture, demonstrating the relationship between music and political action.

1 'They didn't know what they were playing with, look what they got', spoke Jungle Brothers rapper Mike G from the floor of a conference on the state of hip-hop in the late 1990s. In the 20-plus years since it emerged in inner-city New York as an alternative to violence and a way to escape harsh urban realities, hip-hop has become a worldwide musical and cultural force. But the widespread popularity of rap music and hip-hop culture among youth has caught many outside the hip-hop community by surprise. Once considered 'black noise', hip-hop has claimed for itself the role of cultural and political voice of an entire generation of youth.

When hip-hop emerged in New York City in the 1970s, its primary sphere of influence was the youth in the neighborhoods where

"From the margins to mainstream: the political power of hip-hop," by Katina R. Stapleton from *Media, Culture & Society*, Vol. 20, No. 2. Copyright © 1998 by Sage Publications, London.

it evolved. In areas like the Bronx, breakdancers, graffiti artists, MCs (rappers), DJs and fans formed the hip-hop community. Hip-hop scholar Tricia Rose argues that 'alternative local identities were forged in fashions and language, street names, and most important, in establishing neighborhood crews or posses' (Rose, 1994: 34). Crews provided an opportunity for youth to form family-like bonds similar to, but not based on, gang affiliation. Instead of always fighting with fists, hip-hop gave youth the option of fighting with words, art, dance or the ability to produce good beats (Fernando, 1994).

Hip-hop emerged at a time of crisis for youth in urban communities. The situation was no less than a 'deindustrialized meltdown where social alienation, prophetic imagination, and yearning intersect' (Rose, 1994: 21). Hip-hop enabled youth to create their own cultural space within the city that countered the poverty and alienation that surrounded them on a day-to-day basis. As a type of genuine street culture, hip-hop evolved for several years before being discovered by the mass media (Shomari, 1995).

As scholars began to research hip-hop, it became clear that while it developed as an alternative youth culture, hip-hop incorporated many elements of the larger African-American and African cultures (DeMott, 1988; Floyd, 1995; Remes, 1991; Stephens, 1991). One such element is 'playing the dozens', a time-honored tradition in the African-American community. Also known as bragging, boasting, toasting or signifying, the process includes 'ritual insults' in which the speakers test their verbal prowess by seeing who can form the best taunt. Dozens-playing was an integral part of the early rap competitions and has remained a significant element of rap music today.

5   Hip-hop's use of the spoken or sung word to tell stories and teach 'life-lessons' is also part of a tradition among African peoples that goes back to the *griots*, African storytellers who played the important role of oral historians. The griots' role in African communities was to pass down the stories of each generation in song, while imparting knowledge about society. 'Endowed with this much prized oral skill, the griot enjoyed a very respected position within his community, just like many modern-day microphone personalities' (Fernando, 1994: 255). Rappers have become urban griots, using their lyrics to disperse social commentary about what it means to be young and black in the late 20th century (Kuwahara, 1992).

Like more traditional griots, what makes hip-hop artists such successful purveyors of cultural and political information is that they relay messages of importance to youth in a form that they enjoy. Rap music, currently the most visible element of hip-hop, has proven its ability to both capture the ear of those who listen to it for aesthetic reasons and those who look to the genre for deeper meaning. From its rough and tumble forms to the most commercial jams, hip-hop has been able to raise awareness among African-Americans and the general public about the issues that face black youth on a day-to-day basis.

Another strong tradition in African-American music that hip-hop has followed is the use of song to 'tell it like it is' and protest against social injustice (Nelson, 1992; Remes, 1991). In the early 1900s an examination of Negro spirituals as folksongs noted that folksongs were developed out of experience (Krehbiel, 1914). The pathos of what it meant to be a slave was reflected in music of the times. Krehbiel writes, 'as a rule the finest songs are the fruits of suffering undergone and the hope of deliverance from bondage' (Krehbiel, 1914: 26–7). Rochelle Larking (1972) argues that the historic conditions of black Americans will always serve as a basis for protest music. Her 1970s examination of soul music as a form of protest noted that beginning with the blues, black popular music has joined church songs as calls to freedom.

African-Americans, according to the musicologist Jon Spencer, have used secular music such as the blues to reflect the 'hell on earth' which they have been subjected to throughout the ages. These songs, claims Spencer, are no less profound than Old Testament psalms and lamentations. Like these biblical tales of woe, the blues are songs 'that reveal the nitty-gritty details of life as it is lived at the underside of society and the underbelly of history' (Spencer, 1996: xiv). Black music from the blues to funk, soul, jazz and now to hip-hop often shares the hope for deliverance found in Negro folksongs. As noted by Henry Charles (1990), the concept of deliverance is found in many aspects of African-American culture.

The central purpose of this article is to examine how hip-hop culture and music are uniquely situated among youth as a means of political action. While the most obvious means is through lyrical protest, Mark Mattern (1997) provides a larger framework for political action that includes music and the culture in which it develops. In his examination of Cajun music, Mattern suggests three categories of political action that will also form the basis of my analysis: confrontational (protest), deliberative and pragmatic.

Hidden transcripts and confrontational lyrics

10

> Creating culture is not easy. . . . There is a politically conscious, culturally aware, liberated, Black survival kit side to rap music that is being seriously overlooked. (Jackson, 1994)

10

One of the greatest contributions of hip-hop artists to the political landscape is one of protest. Mattern (1997) argues that the use of music to provide protest is a clear example of confrontational political action. Protest music is characterized by objections to injustices and oppressions inflicted on certain individuals and groups. Resistance is key and so are clear distinctions between those being subjugated and those perpetrating the injustice. 'Typically, the intent of protest musicians is to oppose the exploitation and oppression exercised by dominant elites and members of dominant groups' (Mattern, 1997: 2). Mattern finds similar elements of resistance in Cajun music that had been previously found in rap music.

In her seminal study of hip-hop, Tricia Rose (1994) provides an examination of rap music and hip-hop culture as a means to resist the dominant social order. Drawing on the work of James Scott (1990), Rose makes the critical distinction between the means by which those in dominant versus marginalized groups are able to get their messages across. Those in power are represented by dominant public transcripts, which are 'maintained through a wide range of social practices', such as setting the terms of public debate (Rose, 1994: 100). Cut out of the public debate, marginalized groups develop their own resistive or hidden transcripts. These communications take place in disguised form and tend to include critiques of the predominant culture. As one of the most marginalized groups in American history, African-Americans have long fought to be included in public debate. Since its inception, one of the areas found to be most problematic for the expression of African-American culture has been television. While there has been more of an influx of television shows and films that feature African-Americans in recent years, critics argue that blacks are mostly portrayed as comedic objects or criminals (Dates and Barlow, 1990; Greenberg and Brand, 1990). Black youths in particular have looked to the media to find representations of their own lives. Rap music and rap music videos gained in popularity among black youth as they recognized rap as their voice. Rap veteran Chuck D of Public Enemy has been widely quoted as calling rap music the 'Black man's CNN'. In the face of under- and/or misrepresentation in traditional media, black youths have turned to hip-hop as a means to define themselves. In terms of resistance, hip-hop provided a forum from which black youth can portray what it means to be young and black in America and protest against it. In its musical form, hip-hop has been able to form what are termed 'hidden transcripts'. While those from dominant cultural groups have public transcripts, those from marginalized groups often must create their own forum from which they can communicate with each other and transmit messages to the dominant culture. The use of resistive transcripts in rap music serves the dual purpose of using symbolism to critique power holders (Rose, 1994) and providing a dialogic arena in which rappers shape the terms of entry (Skeggs, 1993).

The transcripts found in rap music, while often protesting the treatment of all African-Americans, find black youth, not adults, as their primary audience. Dates and Barlow (1990) suggest that this age division among African-Americans over rap is based in part on perceived class consciousness. They argue that this can be seen in radio programming. Many radio formats reflect a class style, with stations wooing urban contemporary listeners with jazz, soul and traditional R&B while other stations woo black youth with hip-hop influenced R&B and rap music (Dates and Barlow, 1990; Jackson, 1994). In terms of political action, this means that black youth and black adults are finding that they have differing ideas of what protest music should sound like. While 'Say it Loud, I'm Black and I'm Proud' by James Brown and 'Respect' by Aretha Franklin were anthems for blacks who came of age in the 1960s, rap is providing new anthems for black youth of the 1990s.

One of the earliest raps credited with going beyond the boast/party elements of rap music to provide a protest anthem was simply called 'The Message'. Released by Grandmaster Flash and the Furious Five in the early 1980s, 'The Message' captured the angst of black youth growing up in the inner city and lent its name to a type of rap music that would follow.

15   Flash's message that society shouldn't push him because he was   15
close to the edge was something that anyone who had grown up in the ghetto could understand. According to Flash, being raised in the impoverished 'second rate' conditions is what often causes young blacks to harbor deep feelings of anger towards society.

While raps like 'The Message' may have started with GrandMaster Flash in 1982, over the years, the group Public Enemy has brought hard-hitting societal critiques to the forefront of hip-hop. Public Enemy has brought hard-hitting societal critiques to the forefront of hip-hop. Public Enemy's founder and lead rapper Chuck D, writes how PE decided to use their music for social purposes:

> The sociopolitical meaning of Public Enemy came after we decided the group would be called that, because the meaning and the connection of what we were about fit right in. The Black man and woman was considered three-fifths of human being in the Constitution of the United States. Since the government and the general public follow the Constitution, then we must be the enemy. (Chuck D, 1997: 86)

Public Enemy credit their strong commitment to protest to the influences of the Black Panther Party and the Nation of Islam. The combination of PE's political background and their ability to create strong musical and video images allowed them to use their songs to provide powerful statements. Two of the most remembered rap commentaries from PE are '911 is a Joke' and 'Fight the Power'. Even before newspaper and television reporters started telling the general public about the problems inner-city residents had with receiving prompt ambulance service, Public Enemy detailed the situation in rhyme. The raps of nationalist groups such as Public Enemy serve as direct examples of confrontational political action. One criterion of this type of political action is the placement of the group, which is perceived as being oppressed in direct opposition to the oppressors (Mattern, 1997). The resistive transcripts of Public Enemy's song 'Hitler Day', locate people of color in direct opposition to white America.

'Hitler Day' is a critique of America's celebration of Columbus Day. According to the rap, a holiday which celebrates the 'discovery' of America at the expense of its native inhabitants is inherently offensive to people of color.

Chuck D explains that asking native and African-American people to celebrate Columbus Day is analogous to asking Jews to celebrate Adolf Hitler Day. 'For me, that's what Christopher Columbus represents to Black, Brown, and Red nations in North America and throughout the world because he opened the gates for five hundred years of mayhem' (Chuck D, 1997: 198). Other more well known confrontational songs by the group include 'Shut 'Em Down', which encouraged the boycotting of businesses that take from the black community without giving back, and the self-explanatory rap 'Fight the Power'.

Other nation-conscious rappers like Brand-Nubian, X-Clan, Poor Righteous Teachers and KRS-One have provided either direct indictments of the dominant social structure or more hidden critiques (Decker, 1993; Eurie and Spady, 1991; Henderson, 1996). But nation-consciousness in rap music also includes messages of empowerment. Next to Public Enemy, Kris Parker is one of the most well known deliverers of political and social messages to the hip-hop community. Ironically, Kris Parker (KRS-One) began his career as part of Boogie Down Productions (BDP) with the late Scott LaRock. Posing on the cover of 'Criminal Minded with Guns', BDP produced some of the earliest music with a gangster ethic, while at the same time promoting messages of black nationalism, safe sex and the rejection of the drug trade. As a solo artist, KRS-One has cemented his role as a teacher among the hip-hop community. From his 1997 album *I Got Next* KRS-One urges the hip-hop nation to shed what he calls ghetto mentality for one of success. Both Public Enemy and KRS-One represent nation-consciousness based in the 1960s black power movement. Jeffery Decker contends that hip-hop nationalists:

> . . . are most effective when they appropriate popular knowledge from within the black community and exploit its most progressive elements in the process of envisioning a new society. At these moments rappers function in a manner resembling what Antonio Gramsci calls 'organic intellectuals'. (Decker, 1993: 59)

Much of the literature on the presence of confrontational political action in music is implicitly or explicitly indebted to Gramscian Marxism. Organic intellectuals are individuals who hold close ties to their class of origin and whose function is to express class identity and goals (Mattern, 1997). The relationship of the hip-hop artist to a class identity has been clear since hip-hop began. Early hip-hop artists came directly from specific inner-city communities and represented a class of youth facing economic deprivation along with social and political marginalization. Even though the hip-hop community has expanded beyond its core to include youth of all classes, races and cultures, hip-hop artists are expected to remain true to their positions as the representative of black youth. 'Hip-hop nationalists are organic cultural intellectuals to the degree that their activities are directly linked to the everyday struggles of black folk and that their music critically engages the popular knowledge of which they have a part' (Decker, 1993: 59). Henderson (1996) and Decker (1993) note that many prominent examples of hip-hop nationalists are not explicitly linked to 1960s nationalism. The Fugees are among rappers whose vision of nationhood is bounded not by geography, but rather one's link to the African or Afro-Hispanic diaspora. Referring to black youth as black diamonds and pearls, Fugees vocalist Lauren Hill raps, 'If I ruled the world, I'd free all my sons'. This type of nationalism is Afrocentric in nature. Rappers like Queen Latifah look to Mother Africa for inspiration in forming their hip-hop identity.

Gangster rap is another prominent source of confrontational nationalist rap (Decker, 1993). Known for their universal distrust of the police, gangster rappers often use their music to provide graphic indictments of the police and the government interspersed with tales of gangster living. Many gangster rappers prefer to be called realists, because they feel their rap describes what is really going on in the 'hood. With black on black violence being the leading source of death for black youth since 1969, it doesn't seem wrong to many rappers to reflect that in their music (Kitwana, 1994: 41). King George, a member of TRU, contends that this type of realism is more than just talk about killing. 'I'm just relating to what's going on and keeping everybody aware at the same time' (Davis, 1996: 63).

Gender and gangsta-rap

Claims to realism aside, however, there has been widespread debate about whether or not songs that call black women 'bitches' and 'hoes' (whores) as well as songs which detail sex acts, drug sales and extreme violence are negative influences of youth. The portrayal of women and whites in hip-hop music have been special sources of concern (Allison, 1994; Hansen, 1995; Johnson et al., 1995). It would seem obvious that no woman would want to be called a female dog on tape, or have their boyfriends 'Treat 'em like a prostitute'. But while female rappers like M.C. Lyte, Queen Latifah, Yo-Yo and Salt 'n' Pepa began to challenge the conception that only males could rap and shape perceptions of women in the urban community, some female rappers responded by becoming hard-core rappers themselves (Rose, 1994; Skeggs, 1993)

In the late 1990s female rappers have emerged as a force equal to male rappers. Skeggs (1993) argues that if rap in general is used to combat racism and oppression, female artists use rap to battle sexism. While many female hip-hop artists rap about female solidarity, others provide images of women being in control of their sexuality. Skeggs theorizes that for black women, 'sexuality is one of the few cultural resources that they can use for the construction of embodied self worth' (Skeggs, 1993: 310). This notion has not gone unchallenged. Female rappers like Lil' Kim and Foxy Brown have been both vilified and held up for praise for their hard-core attitude and blatantly sexy style. The question 'harlots or heroines?' has followed them since they came on the scene. While supporters celebrate the two female rappers' ability to take charge and proclaim their sexuality, critics challenge their claim to feminism. The Lady of Rage, like many other female rappers, holds conflicting views of artists like Kim and Foxy. "I like Little Kim because she sounds so hard. At first I thought what she was saying was not good because we already got problems as far as women getting recognition and being accepted. I felt that might hinder it a little bit.' But, as Rage notes, 'Sex sells and she's good' (Williams, 1997:63).

Many in the hip-hop community contend that while there are valid concerns about the level of sexual and violent content in hip-hop music, the concern from the media and politicians is not genuine. In stead, negative sentiments towards hip-hop are considered to have racial overtones. Hip-hop artists in attendance at the 1997 Life After Death conference contended that the media and politicians are down on hip-hop because it is a black art from that is being consumed by white youth. The consumption of hip-hop by young whites allows them to become 'ghetto chic' without actually having to live in ghetto conditions (Allison, 1994). Though much of the criticism of hip-hop comes from those outside of the black community, there is a large concern about the tone of rap music within African-American discourse. Rose, who applauds rap for its ability to provide resistive transcripts, lambasts rappers for their sexism. 'I am thoroughly frustrated but not surprised by the apparent need for some rappers to craft elaborate and creative stories about the abuse and domination of young black women' (Rose, 1994: 15).

Likewise, trends toward the inclusion of sex, drugs, violence and, most recently, materialism in rap music have not gone unnoticed or unchallenged by member s of the hip-hop community itself (Life After Death, 1997). Hip-hop conferences held in the aftermath of the violent deaths of favorite sons, Tupac Shakur and the Notorious B.I.G. have looked at whether hip-hop has a social responsibility to the youth that listen to the music. Participants at Life After Death (1997) asked serious questions about the role of violence in the genre. The consensus among panel and audience members seemed to be that in many ways hip-hop is out of control. However, they note—and I agree—that rappers who talk about sex and violence should not be expected to take all the blame. Equal shares of blame should lie with record companies and managers who promote violent/sexual rappers, with the youth who buy these records, and with parents who do not take the time to listen to what their children are listening to. Blame also lies with American society itself, which criticizes rappers for talking about ideals that are in fact embedded in the American way of life, as well as the media who often blow up the violence in hip-hop out of context. A sampling of newspaper articles following the shooting death of Biggie Smalls seems to support claims that in a society where black men are killed in record numbers the media still insist on implying that the rap industry, not guns, kills people (Patillo, 1997).

The fact that rappers reflect aspects of American society and the pursuit of the American dream is important in a political context. Rap has many elements in common with country and hard rock music, but receives more critical attention. 'Rap and country lyrics implicate underclass reality, that the alternative symbol systems have a parallel socio-economic provenience' (Armstrong, 1993: 69). Though both genres are based on somewhat different social realities, they both share a rhetoric of violence. Analyses of press coverage of country and rap have found that while the genres share a tendency towards machismo, they are not treated the same way by the press. The difference, as found by Noe, lies not in the song lyrics, but in the racial lenses through which the songs are interpreted.

> When Ice Cube says, 'Let the suburbs see a nigga inva-sion', many whites interpret that as an incitement to vi-olence. But when Johnny Cash sings, 'Shot a man in Reno/just to watch him die', the public taps its feet and hums. (Noe, 1995: 20)

The irony, says Noe, is that rap is no more amoral than other musical genres, but rappers are being punished for catering to prevalent American themes: sex, violence and materialism.

Setting the boundaries of hip-hop

30 Hip-hop is bigger than any one person's opinion of what it should be, 30 said Chuck D of Public Enemy, now a reporter for the Fox News Channel (Chuck D, 1997: 152). The process of establishing where the boundaries of hip-hop should stand is one of deliberation. Mattern (1997) elaborates on this type of political action. He writes, 'Deliber-ation is a political process and a form of political action in its own right, as well as a necessary preliminary step in forging agreement on common interests and goals for action in other political arenas to ad-dress them' (Mattern, 1997: 7). Mattern uses rap and Cajun music as examples of how differing visions of what a genre should stand for are deliberated within a community. The main point of deliberation within the hip-hop community revolves around the question: 'Has hip-hop gone too far?' Related questions include, but are not limited to: 'Has rap music become too sexual, too violent, and too material-istic?' 'Has hip-hop sold its soul for commercial success?' 'Has hip-hop crossed too far into the territory of other music forms?' 'As a commu-nity, has hip-hop become more suburban and white than black and urban?'

The answers to all these questions are not clear-cut. The very na-ture of hip-hop culture has been one that accommodated many types of people, many types of subject matter, and many types of music. The underlying question, then, is whether or not hip-hop can accommodate varying interests, while still retaining its distinctive urban identity. The presence of intra-group differences and disagreements, and of border zones between different groups, suggests that we consider, at least in some instances, a framework for understanding and action of negotiation, rather than an either-or struggle between opposing forces. Popular music would be viewed in these cases as a site and a medium for disagreement and debate over both intra- and inter-group identity and commitments. This takes shape in a deliberative form of political action (Mattern, 1997:6).

Hip-hop's identity as form of resistance among black youth lies at the heart of deliberation in the hip-hop community. Part of hip-hop's credibility among young blacks lies in its ability to claim that it is an authentic street culture (Powell, 1991). But if hip-hop is 'by the ghetto, for the ghetto', how is the community changed by the fact that it is being played on college campuses across the nation and in the homes of suburban whites? When hip-hop style is being used to sell movies, breath mints, sodas, make-up, fast food, alcohol, clothing, shoes and various other products, one knows that this is a valid concern (Blair, 1993). Similar feelings have been reported from England's hip-hop community. 'Hip-hop's integrity has been prostituted in the pursuit of financial gain', writes a columnist in *Hip-Hop Connection*, one of Britain's hip-hop magazines (Salsa, 1997: 5). Though the author was from England, she accurately summed up concerns that are held across the hip-hop community. Salsa charges that hip-hop is at its best in its resistive mode, but that it has lost its subversiveness due to mainstreaming and commercialization. Bernard-Donais (1994: 133) shares this opinion. 'The very fact that it is covered by an institution like the [*New York*] *Times* suggests that rap has found its way into the canon, and that it has ceased to be the subversive (or in other terms, marginal) form that it had been at one time.'

In the case of hip-hop, the transference from subculture to mainstream has been driven by technological advances. As long as artists performed rap in venues limited to neighborhoods, its marginal status was assured. But as rap music expanded to being mass produced hip-hop spread across the nation (Blair, 1993; Kuwahara, 1992). Hip-hop's influence has not been limited to America. Fans from across the world are able to buy rap music both from traditional record stores and from mail order distribution. The worldwide audience for hip-hop should not be underestimated (Toop, 1991). Hip-hop artists regularly perform to international audiences. Wu Tang Clan and the Fugees are just two examples of what is called global hip-hop. The appeal of hip-hop around the world is based in part on the fact that marginalization, oppression and struggle can be understood by many youth. The love of hip-hop has a universal appeal, agrees Chuck D (1997). He believes that one of the reasons that rap crosses over successfully into mainstream culture is that young whites are able to gain an African-American perspective through the music.

The character of deliberation within the hip-hop community is necessarily shaped by its widespread audience. Stephens (1991) contends that rap provides a 'double-voiced discourse' in which rap crosses racial and geographic boundaries. Hip-hop, writes Stephens, provides a point of intersection where blacks and whites can have a dialogue. Though not always acknowledge in the media, the members of the Hispanic community have also been involved in hip-hop since its inception. In this case, it is urbanity and similar social situations that guide Hispanic contributions to hip-hop (Fernando, 1994; Stephens, 1991). As Rose notes, 'Rap's black cultural address and its focus on marginal identities may appear to be in opposition to its crossover appeal for people from different racial or ethnic groups and social positions', but in reality it suggests 'that rap is a black idiom that prioritizes black culture and that articulates the problems of black urban life in the face of such diverse constituencies' (Rose, 1994: 4).

35 Discussions of hip-hop as a street culture sometimes overlook 35 contributions of college students who have since become hip-hop artists and the strong identification of many black college students with hip-hop culture. Music, if not social class, draws young African-Americans of differing socioeconomic status to hip-hop.

Zillman et al. have looked at the effects of popular rock, non-political rap and radical political rap on African-American and white high-school students. They found that while radical political rap seemed to motivate white students to be more supportive of racial harmony, there was no positive link between political rap and ethnic consciousness or ethnic solidarity among the black students (Zillman et al., 1995). The authors note that this does not imply that message rap does not have an effect on black students. In fact the opposite could be true.

It can be argued that African-American students, in contrast to white students, are massively exposed to rap and that any effect of rap may have manifested itself already prior to exposure. Several additional exposures thus could have influenced white students, especially those who are relatively unfamiliar with radical rap, but not African-American students—because of the informational saturation and its perceptual and evaluative consequences. (Zillman et al., 1995: 21)

Debate about the relative effects of hip-hop on youth is a major area of discussion within the academic community. Instead of concentrating on consciousness, researchers Johnson et al. looked at the effects of violent rap on youth. They found that there was greater acceptance of dating violence among youth exposed to violent rap videos than those exposed to non-violent rap videos or no video at all. In a slightly different experiment they also found that youth exposed to either type of rap video expressed greater desire to be like the materialistic youth portrayed in a scenario than his college-bound friend (Johnson et al., 1995).

Materialism, sexism and violence are points of deliberation among hip-hop artists and fans. Chuck D (1997) recounts the extremely negative reactions he got from African hip-hop fans to the newest incarnations of hip-hop. But as he also notes, the more negative aspects of rap are the easiest to market. 'If you give a fourteen-year-old a choice between a positive video, and a video with tits and ass, or guns and violence, he's going to choose the tits and ass, guns and violence almost every time' (Chuck D, 1997: 33). Researchers have shown that white youth who listen to rap are particularly attracted to its most violent elements. 'The more rappers are packaged as violent black criminals, the bigger their audiences become', writes Ewan Allison (1994: 449).

40   Is this preoccupation with ghetto culture detrimental to youth, 40 black or white? In some ways it is positive, according to Rose, because the ghetto provides a source of social identity for the millions of youth who call it home. Other positive interpretations include the fact that rap has values both because of its brutal honesty and as a point of deliberation. Freestyle rapper Supernatural feels that gangster rap gives other types of rappers more incentive to present the hip-hop experi-

ence from all points of view. Looking at the situation from a slightly different perspective, KRS-One notes that the existence of more than one type of rap exposes the tendency for the public to choose negative over positive. Among participants at Life After Death (1997), the origins of hip-hop were seen as being positive in contrast to more recent developments. Old-school hip-hop artists stressed that hip-hop has strayed too far from its original intentions of combating gang activity to promoting gangster ethics; from promoting black unity to encouraging east coast-west coast feuds; from MC'ing, DJ'ing, breaking, and painting graffiti to simply rapping; from performing for the love of it to performing for money; and from simple boasting to gross exaggerations of one's sexual prowess (Life After Death, 1997; Nia, 1997). Though each of these issues is important to the future of hip-hop, the charge that there has been a dilution of hip-hop as a distinct, protest-based culture and music form is the most political.

Actions speak louder than words

Though the previous discussion in this article has concentrated on both the resistive and deliberative aspects of hip-hop, Mattern suggests music and its related culture also can be used as a basis for pragmatic political action. This type of action, says Mattern, 'begins from the premise of shared political interests. Pragmatic political action occurs when individuals and groups use music to promote awareness of shared interests and to organize collaborative action to address them' (Mattern, 1997: 7). In the past, hip-hop artists have come together for many causes. One prominent example, though considered ill-fated, was the Stop the Violence movement (STV), an attempt to discourage black-on-black crime. Other movements include HEAL (Human Education Against Lies) and the current Rap the Vote project.

Currently there seems to be a resurgence of hip-hop artists attempting to form groups to further the common interests of African-diasporic peoples and/or members of the hip-hop nation. KRS-One, whose song 'Stop the Violence' typified the spirit of the STV movement, has recently started the Temple of Hip-Hop, a non-profit cultural center with the purpose of preserving hip-hop culture. The Zulu nation remains a long-standing conduit of nationalism within the hip-hop community. Many other rap groups and individual artists have taken on specific service projects in order to give back to the community. Perhaps some of the most interesting projects are coming from the ground up. One such project is the Wiseguys, led by Raymond 'Ray Benzino' Scott, president of Boston-based Surrender Records. Using a similar concept to the one of trading a gang for a team, Scott and three friends encouraged former gang rivals to 'trade their hardware for mics'. The project, called Wiseguys, resulted in former gang members coming together to record an album now distributed nationally. Says Scott, 'It becomes a political platform of hypocrisy when you're scared to actually go in and touch the people who are going through the problems' (Walker, 1997: 30–1).

Whether initiated by artists, producers or fans, it is clear that hip-hop has great potential for becoming a major agent of change. All hip-hop needs, according to Chuck D and others, is organization. 'We have to really tie up some areas in the hip-hop Nation: the Zulu Nation, the Rhyme Syndicate, any organization is good. It's just that we have to drop these badges when we come down to dialogue and figure out how to help our people . . .' (Chuck D, 1997: 181). Robert Jackson, author of the *The Last Black Mecca*, believes that an organized hip-hop nation has the potential to be a powerful social and political base within the African-American community: 'The next revolution should be more than televised—it should be political' (Jackson, 1994: 99). The next level for hip-hop, says Jackson, is to organize around a progressive political agenda which would include housing, education and health reform as well as affirmative action and employment.

Music has always been a major source of cultural identity within the African-American community. Rap music is no exception. As part of the larger hip-hop culture, rap music has served to form a cohesive bond among urban youth. Through the mass distribution of hip-hop records and videos, hip-hop has also been able to at least partially erase lines between young people of different socioeconomic backgrounds and vastly different geographic locations. Equally important, hip-hop culture has established itself as a powerful informational tool and means of resistance. It is not an overstatement to say that despite its faults, hip-hop has provided America with one of its only hard-hitting indictments of the social conditions that continue to be a harsh reality for African-American young people.

45   Hip-hop has shown itself to be both the site of political controversy and a means of more than one type of political action. As Mattern notes, confrontational, deliberative and pragmatic political action   45

can occur 'whenever music is produced and consumed', and thus, '[they] should not be viewed as mutually exclusive of each other' (Mattern, 1997: 8). In the case of hip-hop, this is especially true. Rap music, while a significant source of political action within hip-hop, should not be considered its only source. It is its presence within hip-hop community that lends it the context in which resistance emerges. As the hip-hop community looks towards the 21st century, it will be the challenge of hip-hop to define how hip-hop will continue to evolve as a culture and as genuine political force.

References

Allison, E. (1994) 'It's a Black Thing: Hearing How Whites Can't', *Cultural Studies* 8(3): 438–56.

Armstrong, E.G. (1993) 'The Rhetoric of Violence in Rap and Country Music', *Sociological Inquiry* 63(1): 64–83.

Bernard-Donais, M. (1994) 'Jazz, Rock 'n' Roll, Rap and Politics', *Journal of Popular Culture* 28(2): 127–38.

Blair, M.E. (1993) 'The Commercialization of the Rap Music Youth Subculture', *Journal of Popular Culture* 27(3): 21–32.

Charles, H. (1990) *Culture and African American Politics*. Bloomington: Indiana University Press.

Craddock-Willis, A. (1989) 'Rap Music and the Black Musical Tradition', *Radical America* 23(4): 29–38.

D. Chuck (1997) *Fight the Power: Rap, Race and Reality*. New York: Delacorte Press.

Dates, J.L. and W. Barlow (1990) *Split Image: African Americans in the Mass Media*. Washington, DC: Howard University Press.

Davis, T. (1996) 'King George: Tru Royalty', *4080* 35: 63.

Decker, J. (1993) 'The State of Rap: Time and Place in Hip Hop Nationalism', *Social Text* 34: 53–84.

DeMott, D. (1988) 'The Future is Unwritten: Working-Class Youth Cultures in England and America', *Critical Text* 5(1): 42–56.

Eurie, J.D. and J.G. Spady (eds) (1991) *Nation Conscious Rap*. New York: PC International Press.

Fernando, S.H. (1994) *The New Beats: Exploring the Music, Culture, and Attitudes of Hip-Hop Culture*. New York: Harmony Books.

Floyd, S.A. (1995) *The Power of Black Music: Interpreting its History from Africa to the United States*. New York: Oxford University Press.

Greenberg, B. and J. Brand (1994) 'Minorities and the Mass Media: 1970s to 1990s', pp. 273–314 in J. Bryant and D. Zillman (eds) *Media Effects: Advances in Theory and Research*. Hillsdale, NJ: Lawrence Erlbaum Associates.

Hansen, C.H. (1995) 'Predicting Cognitive and Behavioral Effects of Gangsta Rap,' *Basic and Applied Social Psychology* 16(1–2): 43–52.

Henderson, E.A. (1996) 'Black Nationalism and Rap Music', *Journal of Black Studies* 26(3): 308–39.

Jackson, R. (1994) *The Last Black Mecca: Hip-Hop*. Chicago, IL: Research Associates and Frontline Distribution International Inc.

Johnson, J.D., et al. (1995) 'Violent Attitudes and Deferred Academic Aspirations: Deleterious Effects of Exposure to Rap Music', *Basic and Applied Social Psychology* 16(1–2): 27–41.

Kitwana, B. (1994) *The Rap on Gangsta Rap*. Chicago, IL: Third World Press.

Krehbiel, H.E. (1914) *Afro-American Folksongs: A Study in Racial and National Music*. New York and London: G. Shirmer.

Kuwahara, Y. (1992) 'Power to the People Y'all', *Humanity and Society* 16(1): 54–73.

Larking, R. (1972) 'The Soul Message', pp. 92–104 in R. Serge Denisoff and R. Peterson (eds) *The Sounds of Social Change*. Chicago: Rand McNally.

Life After Death: Rap, Reality and Social Responsibility (1997) Harvard University, Cambridge, MA. 3 May.

Mattern, M. (1997) 'Cajun Music, Cultural Revival: Theorizing Political Action in Popular Music', paper prepared for delivery at the 1997 Annual Meeting of the American Political Science Association, Washington, DC.

Nelson, A. (1992) 'The Persistence of Ethnicity in African American Popular Music', *Explorations in Ethnic Studies* 15(1): 47–57.

Nia, M. (1997) 'From God's to Niggas, From Queens to Bitch's: Do Rappers Have An Identity Crisis?', *Beat Down* 5(5): 20.

Noe, D. (1995) 'Parallel Worlds', *Humanist* 55(4): 20–2.

Patillo, M. (1997) 'The Public Eulogy of a Slain Rapper', *The Source* 92: 83.

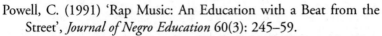

Powell, C. (1991) 'Rap Music: An Education with a Beat from the Street', *Journal of Negro Education* 60(3): 245–59.

Remes, P. (1991) 'Rapping: A Sociolinguistic Study of Oral Tradition', *Anthropological Society of Oxford* 22(2): 129–49.

Rose, T. (1994) *Black Noise: Rap and Black Culture in Contemporary America*. Hanover, NH: Wesleyan University Press.

Salsa, M. (1997) 'Hard Lines', *Hip Hop Connection* 104:5.

Scott, J.C. (1990) *Domination and the Arts of Resistance: Hidden Transcripts*. New Haven, CT: Yale University Press.

Shomari, H. (1995) *From the Underground: Hip Hop Culture As An Agent of Social Change*. Fairwood, NJ: X-Factor Publications.

Skeggs, B. (1993) 'Two Minute Brother: Contestation Through Gender, "Race" and Sexuality', *Innovation* 6(3): 299–322.

Spencer, J.M. (1996) *Re-searching Black Music*. Knoxville: University of Tennessee Press.

Stephens, G. (1991) 'Rap Music's Double-Voiced Discourse', *Journal of Communication Inquiry* 15(2): 70–91.

Toop, D. (1991) *Rap Attack 2: African Rap to Global Hip Hop*. London: Serpent's Tail.

Walker, S. (1997) 'Glocks Down', *The Source* 98: 30–1.

Williams, F. (1997) 'Rage against the Machine', *The Source* 94: 63–6.

Zillman, D., et al. (1995) 'Radical Rap: Does it Further Ethnic Division?', *Basic and Applied Social Psychology* 16(1–2): 1–25.

Questions on Meaning

1. Explain the function of the griot in African culture.
2. What are the main goals of the hip-hop culture? How does it accomplish those goals? In what direction is its development taking it, according to Stapleton's sources?
3. Listen to some blues recordings by artists such as Muddy Waters or Aretha Franklin and compare their lyrics to those of hip-hop artists. Do they have common themes? similar language? How do they differ?

Questions on Rhetorical Strategy and Style

1. Stapleton's article is persuasive that mainstream and intellectual cultures should respect hip-hop. Identify passages that would tend to influence an audience that does not already listen to hip-hop.
2. Stapleton describes the sexism and violence in hip-hop in the same context as her description of hip-hop's positive social protest. What is Stapleton's point in creating the comparison? Does she mean to show the shortcomings of hip-hop artists? Is she arguing that the ghetto conditions justify the sexism and violence?

Writing Assignments

1. Find recordings or videos by one of the hip-hop artists Stapleton names. After you have reviewed the materials, write an essay that explains the artist's political position.
2. Social and political protest were an important part of pop music during the 60s in the work of folk artists such as Joan Baez and Pete Seeger, as well as rock groups such as the Beatles, Jefferson Airplane, and Country Joe and the Fish. Listen to some of those recordings and write an essay that identifies the themes of social protest in the pop mainstream then and now.
3. Poets have often spoken out against injustice. Study some of the rap artists that Stapleton cites and then read some of the works of Robert Bly, Robinson Jeffers, Denise Levertov, Allen Ginsberg, or a comparable white poet writing out of the American experience. Does race matter to white protest poets? If not, what does?

CRITIQUING EDUCATION

Education/testing cartoon
Courtesy of Ann Cleaves.

Questions

1. Political cartoons have the power to condense an often complex argument into a brief statement that makes a claim and implies a whole supporting argument through the use of visuals and text. In you r own words, what is the claim and implied supporting argument made by this cartoon?

2. How does the drawing of the teacher's face, expression, and desktop help convey the argument?

3. What are the implied criteria for "good education" in this cartoon? How does the testing movement fail to meet these criteria?

Reprinted from *Writing Arguments: A Rhetoric With Readings,* Sixth Edition (2004), Addison Wesley Longman.

ME TALK PRETTY ONE DAY

David Sedaris

David Sedaris is considered a master of satire and his readings sell out concert halls across the country. He has a CD entitled David Sedaris at Carnegie Hall. *He read his stories on stage and on the radio, and has had plays produced in New York at La Mama and at Lincoln Center. He has written essays for* Esquire *and* The New Yorker. *His works include* Book of Liz *(2002),* Me Talk Pretty One Day *(2001),* Holidays on Ice *(1998) and* Naked *(1998). He won an Obie Award for a theater production created with his sister, Amy Sedaris, called* One Women Shoe. *Sedaris is a regular contributor to National Public Radio's "This American Life."*

1   At the age of forty-one, I am returning to school and have to think of myself as what my French textbook calls "a true debutant." After paying my tuition, I was issued a student ID, which allows me a discounted entry fee at movie theaters, puppet shows, and Festyland, a far-flung amusement park that advertises with billboards picturing a cartoon stegosaurus sitting in a canoe and eating what appears to be a ham sandwich.

I've moved to Paris with hope of learning the language. My school is an easy ten-minute walk from my apartment, and on the first day of class I arrived early, watching as the returning students greeted one another in the school lobby. Vacations were recounted, and questions were raised concerning mutual friends with names like Kang and Vlatnya. Regardless of their nationalities, everyone spoke in

---

what sounded to me like excellent French. Some accents were better than others, but the students exhibited an ease and confidence I found intimidating. As an added discomfort, they were all young, attractive, and well dressed, causing me to feel not unlike Pa Kettle trapped backstage after a fashion show.

The first day of class was nerve-racking because I knew I'd be expected to perform. That's the way they do it here—it's everybody in the language pool, sink or swim. The teacher marched in, deeply tanned from a recent vacation, and proceeded to rattle off a series of administrative announcements. I've spent quite a few summers in Normandy, and I took a monthlong French class before leaving New York. I'm not completely in the dark, yet I understood only half of what this woman was saying.

"If you have not *meimslsxp* or *lgpdmurct* by this time, then you should not be in this room. Has everyone *apzkiubjxow?* Everyone? Good, we shall begin." She spread out her lesson plan and sighed, saying, "All right, then, who knows the alphabet?"

5   It was startling because (a) I hadn't been asked that question in a   5
while and (b) I realized, while laughing, that I myself did *not* know the alphabet. They're the same letters, but in France they're pronounced differently. I know the shape of the alphabet but had no idea what it actually sounded like.

"Ahh." The teacher went to the board and sketched the letter *a*. "Do we have anyone in the room whose first name commences with an *ahh?*"

Two Polish Annas raised their hands, and the teacher instructed them to present themselves by stating their names, nationalities, occupations, and a brief list of things they liked and disliked in this world. The first Anna hailed from an industrial town outside of Warsaw and had front teeth the size of tombstones. She worked as a seamstress, enjoyed quiet times with friends, and hated the mosquito.

"Oh, really," the teacher said. "How very interesting. I thought that everyone loved the mosquito, but here, in front of all the world, you claim to detest him. How is it that we've been blessed with someone as unique and original as you? Tell us, please."

The seamstress did not understand what was being said but knew that this was an occasion for shame. Her rabbity mouth huffed for breath, and she stared down at her lap as though the appropriate comeback were stitched somewhere alongside the zipper of her slacks.

The second Anna learned from the first and claimed to love sunshine and detest lies. It sounded like a translation of one of those Playmate of the Month data sheets, the answers always written in the same loopy handwriting: "Turn-ons: Mom's famous five-alarm chili! Turnoffs: insecurity and guys who come on too strong!!!!"

The two Polish Annas surely had clear notions of what they loved and hated, but like the rest of us, they were limited in terms of vocabulary, and this made them appear less than sophisticated. The teacher forged on, and we learned that Carlos, the Argentine bandonion player, loved wine, music, and in his words, "making sex with the womens of the world." Next came a beautiful young Yugoslav who identified herself as an optimist, saying that she loved everything that life had to offer.

The teacher licked her lips, revealing a hint of the saucebox we would later come to know. She crouched low for her attack, placed her hands on the young woman's desk, and leaned close, saying, "Oh yeah? And do you love your little war?"

While the optimist struggled to defend herself, I scrambled to think of an answer to what had obviously become a trick question. How often is one asked what he loves in this world? More to the point, how often is one asked and then publicly ridiculed for his answer? I recalled my mother, flushed with wine, pounding the tabletop late one night, saying, "Love? I love a good steak cooked rare. I love my cat, and I love . . ." My sisters and I leaned forward, waiting to hear our names. "Tums," our mother said. "I love Tums."

The teacher killed some time accusing the Yugoslavian girl of masterminding a program of genocide, and I jotted frantic notes in the margins of my pad. While I can honestly say that I love leafing through medical textbooks devoted to severe dermatological conditions, the hobby is beyond the reach of my French vocabulary, and acting it out would only have invited controversy.

When called upon, I delivered an effortless list of things that I detest: blood sausage, intestinal pâtés, brain pudding. I'd learned these words the hard way. Having given it some thought, I then declared my love for IBM typewriters, the French word for *bruise,* and my electric floor waxer. It was a short list, but still I managed to mispronounce *IBM* and assign the wrong gender to both the floor waxer and the typewriter. The teacher's reaction led me to believe that these mistakes were capital crimes in the country of France.

15   "Were you always this *palicmkrexis?*" she asked. "Even a *fiuscrzsa* 15
ticiwelmun knows that a typewriter is feminine."

    I absorbed as much of her abuse as I could understand, think-
ing—but not saying—that I find it ridiculous to assign a gender to an
inanimate object incapable of disrobing and making an occasional
fool of itself. Why refer to crack pipe or Good Sir Dishrag when these
things could never live up to all that their sex implied?

    The teacher proceeded to belittle everyone from German Eva,
who hated laziness, to Japanese Yukari, who loved paintbrushes and
soap. Italian, Thai, Dutch, Korean, and Chinese—we all left class fool-
ishly believing that the worst was over. She'd shaken us up a little, but
surely that was just an act designed to weed out the deadweight. We
didn't know it then, but the coming months would teach us what it
was like to spend time in the presence of a wild animal, something
completely unpredictable. Her temperament was not based on a series
of good and bad days but, rather, good and bad moments. We soon
learned to dodge chalk and protect our heads and stomachs whenever
she approached us with a question. She hadn't yet punched anyone,
but it seemed wise to protect ourselves against the inevitable.

    Though we were forbidden to speak anything but French, the
teacher would occasionally use us to practice any of her five fluent
languages.

    "I hate you," she said to me one afternoon. Her English was flaw-
less. "I really, really hate you." Call me sensitive, but I couldn't help
but take it personally.

20   After being singled out as a lazy *kfdtinvfm,* I took to spending 20
four hours a night on my homework, putting in even more time
whenever we were assigned an essay. I suppose I could have gotten by
with less, but I was determined to create some sort of identity for
myself: David the hard worker, David the cut-up. We'd have one of
those "complete this sentence" exercises, and I'd fool with the thing
for yours, invariably settling on something like "A quick run around
the lake? I'd love to! Just give me a moment while I strap on my
wooden leg." The teacher, through word and action, conveyed the
message that if this was my idea of an identity, she wanted nothing to
do with it.

    My fear and discomfort crept beyond the borders of the class-
room and accompanied me out onto the wide boulevards. Stopping
for a coffee, asking directions, depositing money in my bank account:

these things were out of the question, as they involved having to speak. Before beginning school, there'd been no shutting me up, but now I was convinced that everything I said was wrong. When the phone rang, I ignored it. If someone asked me a question, I pretended to be deaf. I knew my fear was getting the best of me when I started wondering why they don't sell cuts of meat in vending machines.

My only comfort was the knowledge that I was not alone. Huddled in the hallways and making the most of our pathetic French, my fellow students and I engaged in the sort of conversation commonly overheard in refugee camps.

"Sometime me cry alone at night."

"That be common for I, also, but be more strong, you. Much work and someday you talk pretty. People start love you soon. Maybe tomorrow, okay."

25   Unlike the French class I had taken in New York, here there was   25 no sense of competition. When the teacher poked a shy Korean in the eyelid with a freshly sharpened pencil, we took no comfort in the fact that, unlike Hyeyoon Cho, we all knew the irregular past tense of the verb *to defeat*. In all fairness, the teacher hadn't meant to stab the girl, but neither did she spend much time apologizing, saying only, "Well, you should have been *vkkdyo* more *kdeynfulh*."

Over time it became impossible to believe that any of us would ever improve. Fall arrived and it rained every day, meaning we would now be scolded for the water dripping from our coats and umbrellas. It was mid-October when the teaching singled me out, saying, "Every day spent with you is like having a cesarean section." And it struck me that, for the first time since arriving in France, I could understand every word that someone was saying.

Understanding doesn't mean that you can suddenly speak the language. Far from it. It's a small step, nothing more, yet its rewards are intoxicating and deceptive. The teacher continued her diatribe and I settled back, bathing in the subtle beauty of each new curse and insult.

"You exhaust me with your foolishness and reward my efforts with nothing but pain, do you understand me?"

The world opened up, and it was with great joy that I responded, "I know the thing that you speak exact now. Talk me more, you, plus, please, plus."

Questions on Meaning

1. Have you ever been in a situation where you could not fluently speak a language and thus felt awkward and powerless? What was this experience like for you? Explain in detail. How did you manage to maintain your sense of identity?

2. Explain the attitude of the teacher. It appears plainly rude, but it is also a reflection of more complicated and problematic traditions. As students, what do you make of the teacher's behavior?

3. What understanding does the author come to at the end? What "world opened up" and why was it joyful?

Questions on Rhetorical Strategy and Style

1. An important characteristic of this essay is its humor. What manner of humor is it? How does it serve to advance the author's perspective?

2. When the teacher asks the students if they know the alphabet, the author realizes that he does not. What is the symbolic significance of this reference to the basic units of language?

3. A good portion of the essay is devoted to the two Annas, the Argentine bandonion player, and the Yugoslav optimist. What purpose do they serve the essay? Discuss each one separately.

Writing Assignments

1. The author's experience might be unusual in some respects, but in one sense, it is a typical story of the return of a so-called nontraditional student. If you have a similar experience, write an essay describing it. If you know such a student, interview him or her and write a profile of that person's experiences.

2. The essay is an example of a literacy narrative. These are essays that describe someone's experience with acquiring a literacy that results in empowerment. A famous example of such a narrative is the essay "Learning to Read and Write" by Frederick Douglass. Write your own narrative of how you came to be a reader and a writer. In your essay, detail specific experiences that illustrate your story.

ENGLISH LESSON IN CALIFORNIA

Gregory Rodriguez

Gregory Rodriguez (1966-) was born in Los Angeles and graduated from the University of California at Berkeley with a degree in Religious Studies. He is a contributing editor for Los Angeles Magazine *and the* Los Angeles Times *Opinion section as well as an associate editor at Pacific News Service. Also, he is a research fellow at the Pepperdine Institute for Public Policy, a fellow at the New America Foundation in Washington, D. C., and a senior research fellow at the Alta California Research Center. In this article from the April 20, 1998 issue of* The Nation, *Rodriguez writes about the "English for the Children" program and the threat it poses to bilingual education.*

1   Early this past February, thousands of bilingual teachers and advocates descended upon San Jose, California, to attend what may wind up being the very last annual conference of the California Association of Bilingual Educators. CABE, as the group is known, is facing the greatest threat to its controversial profession since the advent of bilingual education a quarter-century ago.

Two months from now, on June 2, the California electorate will be casting votes on "English for the Children," a popular ballot initiative that would effectively put an end to bilingual education in California's public schools. But while CABE and its members will actively fight the measure they refer to simply as the Unz initiative, after conservative software entrepreneur Ron Unz, who is sponsoring the campaign, the will not be on the front lines of the battle. Strategists for

---

"English Lesson in California" by Gregory Rodriguez, published in *The Nation*, April 20, 1998.

the "No on Unz" campaign have decided not only that bilingual teachers don't make the best spokespeople for the cause but that debating the efficacy of the teaching method is counterproductive. Indeed, until Election Day, the No on Unz campaign will seek to avoid mentioning bilingual education at all.

For a generation, while federal law has required schools to provide special language instruction to assist English learners in obtaining an equal education, it has never mandated the form that this assistance must take. Since the seventies, a mixture of blind faith and administrative arrogance has not only kept bilingual education afloat but made it unassailable. In their zeal to protect the program from any challenges, its ardent supporters have also consistently opposed any attempts to reform it. California's powerful teachers' unions—one of the Democratic Party's strongest constituencies—made the issue a mainstay of that state's liberal agenda.

Because activists had early on identified bilingual education as the primary Latino civil rights issue, the equivalent of what busing was to blacks, foes and doubters of the program were routinely branded as racists. Unfortunately, this defensive posture insured that bilingual lobbyists were more concerned with preserving the program than making sure it was benefiting the children it served.

5 For decades, bilingual education has been debated in cultural rather than pedagogical terms, its supporters citing the benefits of maintaining children's ethnic and linguistic heritage, its opponents insisting that immigrants should learn English and fretting that today's immigrants are not as eager to assimilate as their predecessors. Lost in this racialized hubbub was the only question that should have mattered: Is bilingual education helping or hurting limited-English speakers in U.S. public schools? Unfortunately, after a generation of politicized debate over the issue, there is still no definitive answer. There are plenty of studies showing that bilingual education works if implemented well. There are also studies proving that English immersion works when properly implemented. Last year, the National Research council released a report calling most evaluations of bilingual-education programs worthless. The report claimed not only that politicization of the issue has hampered reliable research but also that scholarly efforts to prove the superiority of either English-only or bilingual education are pointless. Instead, the report's authors urged, studies should focus on identifying the teaching methods that work

best in specific communities, according to local needs and available resources.

Despite its name, bilingual education has nothing to do with bilingualism. The vast majority of bilingual programs in California use "early-exit transitional bilingual education," in which students are expected to make a transition into "mainstream English" classes after three or four years of instruction in their primary language. Early-exit programs are designed to teach children how to read and write in their native language in the belief that they will be better able to learn a second language, in this case English.

In California, even bilingual-education supporters don't think the current system is working. While defending the integrity of primary-language instruction, CABE concedes that perhaps 10 percent or fewer of the state's bilingual programs are well implemented. A perennial shortage of bilingual teachers is one of the main reasons. California currently needs more than 20,000 additional bilingual teachers to serve the state's 1.4 million limited-English students adequately. Supporters blame the shortage on the lack of political and fiscal support for the program.

But even in Los Angeles, the second-largest school district in the country, which has fully supported bilingual education for years—both financially and politically—there is no evidence that the program is achieving its stated goals. Despite the controversy that has engulfed the program since its inception, the Los Angeles Unified School District administrators have never found it necessary to compile reliable data to evaluate it. School board members and administrators have usually relied on rhetoric to defend the widely misunderstood program. Instead of referring to data to prove success, one district administrator took pleasure in warning that "if we got rid of bilingual education, we'd be creating a huge underclass."

The absence of persuasive evidence has left school districts open to equally insubstantial charges by the "English for the Children" campaign that bilingual education is an utter failure. But because the state and federal governments have spent hundreds of millions of dollars in public money implementing the controversial program over three decades, the burden of proof would seem to lie with its proponents.

The least subjective study to date on the efficacy of bilingual education was recently released by two young Mexican-American economists. Rather than compare test scores and measure the relative efficiency of opposing pedagogical methods, Mark Lopez of the University of Maryland and Marie Mora of New Mexico State University decided to measure the effect bilingual education has on the earnings of Latinos. They found that first- and second-generation Latinos who attended a bilingual-education program earn significantly less than their otherwise similar peers who received monolingual English instruction.

In fighting against "English for the Children," advocates of bilingual education attack the measure as an untested, one-size-fits-all mandate that robs both local school districts and parents of their right to choose which teaching methods are appropriate for their children. It is of course ironic that liberal activists have chosen the traditionally conservative themes of arguing for greater local control and against big-government intervention.

This argument and others are marshaled against a critical political factor: Proponents of bilingual education have lost crucial portions of their core support groups. Today, as in the past, bilingual advocates can rely on both teachers' unions and Latino advocacy organizations to defend their cause. (Both the California Teachers Association and the Mexican American Legal Defense and Educational Fund are actively opposing the initiative.) But whereas in past years leaders of such associations were commonly assumed to be representative of the people for whom they spoke, recent polls and surveys indicate otherwise. Unquestioning support for bilingual education has eroded among teachers. Last November, the rank and file of United Teachers Los Angeles voted on whether the union should endorse "English for the Children." Even though the mass of U.T.L.A.'s executive leadership urged a vote against the referendum, 47 percent of the members supported it.

When "English for the Children" surfaced last May, it looked like the logical political descendant of recent state campaigns against illegal immigration and affirmative action—the newest target for the state's disproportionately large Anglo electorate. Presumably, much of the white electorate, led by conservatives and anti-immigrant activists, would line up to support the initiative, while liberals and Latinos would reject it. But a different political dynamic has emerged. Neither the Latino political leadership nor the state Republican Party has spearheaded a campaign for or against the initiative.

Surprisingly to some, early surveys by the *Los Angeles Times* and the Field Poll showed that Latino registered voters supported the initiative by a wide margin. That evidence alone was enough to make members of California's state Latino Legislative Caucus rethink their strategy on bilingual education. Although not long ago the state's Latino leadership would have gone down fighting any proposal that sought to overhaul bilingual education, no one is now willing to dedicate large amounts of money or political capital to defeat an initiative that may prove popular among Latinos. Many longtime observers have predicted that the Latino vote will be split. Monica Lozano, associate publisher of the daily *La Opinion*, believes that Latinos will vote 60 percent to 40 percent in favor of the initiative. The most recent Field Poll, released in late March, showed that likely Latino voters supported it by a margin of 60 percent to 34 percent. According to a survey by the Center for the Study of Los Angeles at Loyola Marymount University, L.A.'s Latino leadership does not consider defending bilingual education to be among the top five cutting-edge issues facing Latinos. Political scientist Fernando Guerra, who conducted the survey, says the issues has been steadily declining in importance on the Latino political agenda.

15   Meanwhile, the leadership of the state Republican Party has distanced itself from the initiative so as not to open the G.O.P. to more charges of immigrant- or Latino-bashing. State G.O.P. chairman Michael Schroeder has defied both a rank-and-file vote supporting the Unz initiative and his own distaste for bilingual education to publicly distance the party from the ballot measure. This is a notably cautious response from the man who was Robert Dornan's lawyer in the ill-fated battle to invalidate Representative Loretta Sanchez's 1996 victory over Dornan in Orange County's 46th Congressional District. Nor will Governor Pete Wilson utter a word on the initiative, in part out of personal dislike for Ron Unz, who impertinently ran against the incumbent Governor in the 1994 Republican primary on a pro-immigrant platform.

Indeed, the political no-man's land into which this initiative has descended is strangely reflective of its sponsor, the libertarian physicist-cum-software-designer millionaire, who does not include immigrant-bashing in his portfolio. While Wilson was riding the anti-immigrant wave of Proposition 187 to re-election, Unz was a featured speaker at a 70,000-strong pro-immigrant rally in October 1994.

But the wide appeal of the Unz initiative doesn't necessarily make it good policy. No matter what the issue, California's initiative process is usually the worst way to solve complex problems. By nature, voter initiatives are the legislative process least amenable to political compromise. As such, "English for the Children" could still become the instrument by which an overwhelmingly Anglo electorate asserts its displeasure with the state's Latino-bound demographic metamorphosis. If passed, "English for the Children" will require that most of California's limited-English students be taught in English. These students will have no more than one year of "sheltered English" instruction—teachers using simple, accessible language—before being moved into regular classrooms. No research supports the premise of a one-year sheltered English approach. The broad and sometimes imprecise wording of the initiative leaves many aspects of the state's language-learning policy unclear, even outright confusing. For instance, there is no plan to deal with children unprepared to make the transition to mainstream classes. While the ballot measure seems to make exceptions available to parents who want their children to remain in bilingual programs, it is unclear what criteria will enable them to receive a waiver.

Administrators at L.A. Unified, the largest school district in California and home to close to a quarter of the state's limited-English children, are predicting chaos if the ballot measure passes. In a preliminary review, district staff have painted a picture of a school district torn asunder, one with test scores dropping even lower than their current unacceptable lows. The lack of a pedagogical plan other than the one year of "sheltered English" makes it unclear how and what educators will teach newly transitioned students, let alone those whose bilingual programs collapse under them. It is also unclear how and what educators will teach newly transitioned students, let alone those whose bilingual programs collapse under them. It is also unclear what fiscal effects the Unz measure will have on the 682,000-student district.

Members of the state Latino Legislative Caucus have been trying to reform the program to take the urgency out of the Unz initiative. There is near-universal consensus that bilingual education desperately needs repairs. Once-intransigent bilingual supporters are willing to make significant changes in order to save the program. Echoes of "Mend it, don't end it" are in the air. Before officially voting to oppose the Unz initiative, a majority of the Los Angeles School Board publicly acknowledged the shortcomings of the district's bilingual-education programs.

20   Political scientist Guerra believes that the No on Unz campaign   20
may still be able to garner a majority of Latino votes if it is able to reframe the ballot measure as anti-immigrant or anti-Latino. "Even if it's not true, if they paint the initiative with a broad stroke as being brought to you by the same people who gave us Propositions 187 and 209, at least 60 percent of Latinos will vote against it," he says. But playing the race card could just as easily backfire. Arturo Vargas, executive director of the National Association of Latino Elected and Appointed Officials, thinks a racialized campaign may have strategically negative unintended consequences. "The [Latino] leadership was using race in 1994 and 1996. That rhetoric may have driven up the yes vote," he says. "If you get up to say it's racist, you tend to lose credibility."

Going into the last leg of the campaign and still riding high in the polls, Unz may find his hubris to be the only force that can sink his campaign. Having said from the start that a victory for his ballot measure would be morally hollow without Latino support, he has been lax in creating a media campaign to appeal to voters. But some institutional heavy hitters are taking aim at what is officially termed Proposition 227: The White House is expected to come out against the measure, as is the Spanish-language television network Univision (whose C.E.O. was one of the biggest donors to Governor Wilson's re-election campaign). The No on Unz campaign, run by veteran Democratic political consultant Richie Ross, may both outspend and outstrategize Unz in the final weeks of the campaign. Ross is planning a sophisticated multimedia attack, and Unz says he may not have the money for production of television ads.

Pass or fail, the challenge to primary-language instruction can at least claim to have made bilingual advocates more open to compromise. "Our bilingual program is not the greatest in the world," said L.A. School Board member Barbara Boudreaux with striking candor. "This may be a wake-up call for us to do the right thing for all the children we serve." Board member David Tokofsky went a step further, calling on colleagues to order an immediate review of the district's instructional programs for non-native speakers and to undertake any necessary reforms. Vicky Castro, a school board member who supports bilingual education, acknowledged that her district's past inflexible approach to the program had helped fuel a backlash against it. Indeed, Ron Unz claims that the catalyst for the measure was the protest that immigrant Latino parents staged two years ago at Ninth Street Elementary School near downtown L.A. after school administrators rebuffed requests for additional English-language instruction for their children. "English for the Children" has effectively upgraded the urgency of the long-running controversy over bilingual education. The newfound openness to reform evident among supporters of bilingual instruction may have meant a great deal two years ago. Now, it may prove too little, too late. Their last-minute politicking may wind up being the meaningless prelude to a disaster of their own making.

Questions on Meaning

1. In this article, the author explains that bilingual education in California is losing support. According to Rodriguez, what has caused that support to erode, and what is its social and cultural significance?
2. What is "English for the Children"? What are some of the concerns surrounding this initiative, and what are those concerns based on? What lesson does Rodriguez refer to in the title?

Questions on Rhetorical Strategy and Style

1. Who is the audience for this article? What kind of evidence does Rodriguez rely upon? How does his use of evidence convey his sense of audience?
2. How would you describe the tone of the article? What is the author's stance toward his subject? Is he arguing, or merely reporting? Explain.

Writing Assignments

1. What does the subject of this article have to do with shifting attitudes toward affirmative action?
2. Write an essay about a time when you had to learn a difficult subject in school. In your essay, try to imagine what it might be like to have to learn that subject in another language. What sorts of obstacles would you have to overcome?

THEME FOR ENGLISH B

Langston Hughes

Langston Hughes (1902–1967) was born in Joplin, Missouri, and grew up in Kansas and Ohio. A poet from childhood, he attended Columbia University to study engineering but dropped out. In 1923, Hughes shipped out on a freighter to Africa, and later to Italy and France, Russia and Spain. He eventually returned to college at Lincoln University, from which he was graduated in 1929. In his long career as a writer, Hughes published sixteen books of poetry.

1   The instructor said,

> Go home and write
> a page tonight.
> And let that page come out of you—
5   Then, it will be true.

I wonder if it's that simple?
I am twenty-two, colored, born in Winston-Salem.
I went to school there, then Durham, then here
to this college on the hill above Harlem.
10 I am the only colored student in my class.

The steps from the hill lead down into Harlem,
through a park, then I cross St. Nicholas,
Eighth Avenue, Seventh, and I come to the Y,
the Harlem Branch Y, where I take the elevator
15 up to my room, sit down, and write this page:

It's not easy to know what is true for you or me
at twenty-two, my age. But I guess I'm what

"Theme for English B," by Langston Hughes, reprinted from *The Collected Poems of Langston Hughes,* edited by Arnold Rampersad and David Roessel, 1951, Alfred A. Knopf.

I feel and see and hear. Harlem, I hear you:
hear you, hear me—we too—you, me, talk on this page,
20 (I hear New York, too.) Me—who?

Well, I like to eat, sleep, drink, and be in love.
I like to work, read, learn, and understand life.
I like a pipe for a Christmas present,
or records—Bessie, bop, or Bach.
25 I guess being colored doesn't make me *not* like
the same things other folks like who are other races.
So will my page be colored that I write?
Being me, it will not be white.
But it will be
30 a part of you, instructor.
You are white—
yet a part of me, as I am a part of you.
That's American.
Sometimes perhaps you don't want to be a part of me
35 Nor do I often want to be a part of you.
But we are, that's true,
I guess you learn from me—
although you're older—and white—
and sometimes more free.

40 This is my page for English B.

Questions on Meaning

1. This poem ironically comments on a teacher's assignment. What clues do you get that the poet wants you to understand that the teacher doesn't know what he or she is asking for with the instructions to let a page "come out of you" in order to be true?
2. Ask your teacher what he or she would hope or expect to see from students who write in response to an assignment like the one that begins this poem.

Questions on Rhetorical Strategy and Style

1. Why does the poet divide the verse paragraphs where he does? (Hint: "for no good reason" is the wrong answer.) Explain.
2. Rewrite this poem, substituting your own places and names for those that Hughes supplies. Then comment on the differences between you and the poet. Are they a factor of race, gender, age, social class, region, or something else?

Writing Assignments

1. Describe a writing assignment that worked well for you or a writing experience that was postive. Explain what about the assignment helped you most. Describe your writing processes including such features as planning, researching, drafting, consulting with others, or anything else that seems relevant.
2. The poem gives extremely condensed descriptions of important preferences and experiences. Choose one of the poem's statements (e.g., "I wonder if it's that simple," "I am twenty-two," "It's not easy to know what is true"), and write an essay exploring the meaning of the statement in your life.

FROM: THE SCHOOL DAYS OF AN INDIAN GIRL

Zitkala-Sa

Zitkala-Sa (1876–1938) was born as Gertrude Simmons on the Pine Ridge Reservation in South Dakota to a full-blooded Sioux mother and a white father who abandoned the family. At the age of eight she enrolled in a Quaker boarding school for American Indians, later attending normal (teacher-training) school and finally accepting scholarships to Earlham College in Indiana, where she excelled in oratory. An accomplished musician, Zitkala-Sa also attended the Boston Conservatory of Music before beginning a brief teaching career at the Carlisle Indian School. The exploitation of student labor at the school, as well as the suppression of native custom and language, led her to write several articles critical of the school for Atlantic Monthly *and* Harper's Monthly *under the pen name Zitkala-Sa (Red Bird). After marrying another mixed-blood Sioux, Raymond Bonnin, Zitkala-Sa became an activist with the Society of American Indians and edited* American Indian Magazine. *Her collection of personal narratives and tribal legends, titled* American Indian Stories, *was published in 1921; she also wrote the libretto for an opera,* Sun Dance. *In the following selection Zitkala-Sa recounts the terrors and humiliations undergone by young American Indian children at the hands of white missionaries determined to lead them "from savagery to civilization."*

Excerpt from "The School Days of an Indian Girl," reprinted from *Atlantic*, 85, February, 1900, pp. 185–194.

I. The Land of Red Apples

There were eight in our party of bronzed children who were going East with the missionaries. Among us were three young braves, two tall girls, and we three little ones, Judéwin, Thowin, and I.

We had been very impatient to start on our journey to the Red Apple Country, which, we were told, lay a little beyond the great circular horizon of the Western prairie. Under a sky of rosy apples we dreamt of roaming as freely and happily as we had chased the cloud shadows on the Dakota plains. We had anticipated much pleasure from a ride on the iron horse, but the throngs of staring palefaces disturbed and troubled us.

On the train, fair women, with tottering babies on each arm, stopped their haste and scrutinized the children of absent mothers. Large men, with heavy bundles in their hands, halted near by, and riveted their glassy blue eyes upon us.

I sank deep into the corner of my seat, for I resented being watched. Directly in front of me, children who were no larger than I hung themselves upon the backs of their seats, with their bold white faces toward me. Sometimes they took their forefingers out of their mouths and pointed at my moccasined feet. Their mothers, instead of reproving such rude curiosity, looked closely at me, and attracted their children's further notice to my blanket. This embarrassed me, and kept me constantly on the verge of tears.

I sat perfectly still, with my eyes downcast, daring only now and then to shoot long glances around me. Chancing to turn to the window at my side, I was quite breathless upon seeing one familiar object. It was a telegraph pole which strode by at short paces. Very near my mother's dwelling, along the edge of a road thickly bordered with wild sunflowers, some poles like these had been planted by white men. Often I had stopped, on my way down the road, to hold my ear against the pole, and, hearing its low moaning, I used to wonder what the paleface had done to hurt it. Now I sat watching for each pole that glided by to be the last one.

In this way I had forgotten my uncomfortable surroundings, when I heard one of my comrades call out my name. I saw the missionary standing very near, tossing candies and gums into our midst. This amused us all, and we tried to see who could catch the most of the sweet-meats. The missionary's generous distribution of candies was impressed upon my memory by a disastrous result which followed. I had caught more than my share of candies and gums, and soon after our arrival at the school I had a chance to disgrace myself, which, I am ashamed to say, I did.

Though we rode several days inside of the iron horse, I do not recall a single thing about our luncheons.

It was night when we reached the school grounds. The lights from the windows of the large buildings fell upon some of the icicled trees that stood beneath them. We were led toward an open door, where the brightness of the lights within flooded out over the heads of the excited palefaces who blocked the way. My body trembled more from fear than from the snow I trod upon.

Entering the house, I stood close against the wall. The strong glaring light in the large whitewashed room dazzled my eyes. The noisy hurrying of hard shoes upon a bare wooden floor increased the whirring in my ears. My only safety seemed to be in keeping next to the wall. As I was wondering in which direction to escape from all this confusion, two warm hands grasped me firmly, and in the same moment I was tossed high in midair. A rosy-cheeked paleface woman caught me in her arms. I was both frightened and insulted by such trifling. I stared into her eyes, wishing her to let me stand on my own feet, but she jumped me up and down with increasing enthusiasm. My mother had never made a plaything of her wee daughter. Remembering this I began to cry aloud.

10   They misunderstood the cause of my tears, and placed me at a   10 white table loaded with food. There our party were united again. As I did not hush my crying, one of the older ones whispered to me, "Wait until you are alone in the night."

It was very little I could swallow besides my sobs, that evening.

"Oh, I want my mother and my brother Dawée! I want to go to my aunt!" I pleaded; but the ears of the palefaces could not hear me.

From the table we were taken along an upward incline of wooden boxes, which I learned afterward to call a stairway. At the top was a quiet hall, dimly lighted. Many narrow beds were in one straight line down the entire length of the wall. In them lay sleeping brown faces, which peeped just out of the coverings. I was tucked into bed with one of the tall girls, because she talked to me in my mother tongue and seemed to soothe me.

I had arrived in the wonderful land of rosy skies, but I was not happy, as I had thought I should be. My long travel and the bewildering sights had exhausted me. I fell asleep, heaving deep, tired sobs. My tears were left to dry themselves in streaks, because neither my aunt nor my mother was near to wipe them away.

II The Cutting of My Long Hair

15   The first day in the land of apples was a bitter-cold one; for the snow   15
still covered the ground, and the trees were bare. A large bell rang for breakfast, its loud metallic voice crashing through the belfry overhead and into our sensitive ears. The annoying clatter of shoes on bare floors gave us no peace. The constant clash of harsh noises, with an undercurrent of many voices murmuring an unknown tongue, made a bedlam within which I was securely tied. And though my spirit tore itself in struggling for its lost freedom, all was useless.

A paleface woman, with white hair, came up after us. We were placed in a line of girls who were marching into the dining room. These were Indian girls, in stiff shoes and closely clinging dresses. The small girls wore sleeved aprons and shingled hair. As I walked noiselessly in my soft moccasins, I felt like sinking to the floor, for my blanket had been stripped from my shoulders. I looked hard at the Indian girls, who seemed not to care that they were even more immodestly dressed than I, in their tightly fitting clothes. While we marched in, the boys entered at an opposite door. I watched for the three young braves who came in our party. I spied them in their ranks, looking as uncomfortable as I felt.

A small bell was tapped, and each of the pupils drew a chair from under the table. Supposing this act meant they were to be seated, I pulled out mine and at once slipped into it from one side. But when I turned my head, I saw that I was the only one seated, and all the rest at our table remained standing. Just as I began to rise, looking shyly around to see how chairs were to be used, a second bell was sounded. All were seated at last, and I had to crawl back into my chair again. I heard a man's voice at one end of the hall, and I looked around to see him. But all the others hung their heads over their plates. As I glanced at the long chain of tables, I caught the eyes of a paleface woman upon me. Immediately I dropped my eyes, wondering why I was so keenly watched by the strange woman. The man ceased his mutterings, and then a third bell was tapped. Every one picked up his knife and fork and began eating. I began crying instead, for by this time I was afraid to venture anything more.

But this eating by formula was not the hardest trial in that first day. Late in the morning, my friend Judéwin gave me a terrible warning. Judéwin knew a few words of English; and she had overheard the paleface woman talk about cutting our long, heavy hair. Our mothers had taught us that only unskilled warriors who were captured had their hair shingled by the enemy. Among our people, short hair was worn by mourners, and shingled hair by cowards!

We discussed our fate some moments, and when Judéwin said, "We have to submit, because they are strong," I rebelled.

"No, I will not submit! I will struggle first!" I answered.

I watched my chance, and when no one noticed I disappeared. I crept up the stairs as quietly as I could in my squeaking shoes,—my moccasins had been exchanged for shoes. Along the hall I passed, without knowing whither I was going. Turning aside to an open door, I found a large room with three white beds in it. The windows were covered with dark green curtains, which made the room very dim. Thankful that no one was there, I directed my steps toward the corner farthest from the door. On my hands and knees I crawled under the bed, and cuddled myself in the dark corner.

From my hiding place I peered out, shuddering with fear whenever I heard footsteps near by. Though in the hall loud voices were calling my name, and I knew that even Judéwin was searching for me, I did not open my mouth to answer. Then the steps were quickened and the voices became excited. The sounds came nearer and nearer. Women and girls entered the room. I held my breath, and watched them open closed doors and peep behind large trunks. Some one threw up the curtains, and the room was filled with sudden light. What caused them to stoop and look under the bed I do not know. I remember being dragged out, though I resisted by kicking and scratching wildly. In spite of myself, I was carried downstairs and tied fast in a chair.

I cried aloud, shaking my head all the while until I felt the cold blades of the scissors against my neck, and heard them gnaw off one of my thick braids. Then I lost my spirit. Since the day I was taken from my mother I had suffered extreme indignities. People had stared at me. I had been tossed about in the air like a wooden puppet. And now my long hair was shingled like a coward's! In my anguish I moaned for my mother, but no one came to comfort me. Not a soul reasoned quietly with me like my own mother used to do: for now I was only one of many little animals driven by a herder.

Questions on Meaning

1. Zitkala-Sa recalls two particular indignities to which she was subjected during her journey: being stared at by the white people on the train and being tossed in the air by the missionary teacher. Why is she offended by these things? Why are the white people unable to understand her offense?

2. How does the author emphasize the significance of clothing to her people? How does she react to the clothing worn by the children at the school?

3. When her hair is cut off, the author states that she lost her spirit. In what ways is she speaking metaphorically? In what ways might she be speaking literally, given her traditions?

Questions on Rhetorical Strategy and Style

1. This narrative is told from the point of view of a child. Find several passages in which this point of view is evident and explain their significance to the story.

2. Zitkala-Sa describes certain features of the boarding school in great detail: the bright lights of the main room at night, the rows of beds in the dormitory, and the room in which she hides. Why does she focus on these details? Of what significance are they to the little girl?

Writing Assignments

1. Recall an incident from your childhood in which you found yourself in unfamiliar surroundings. Write a narrative describing your response to the place, using the kind of detail found in this story.

2. Read about the Christian boarding schools established in the late nineteenth century to educate American Indian children. Write an essay describing the schools, focusing on the motivation of the missionaries, the treatment of the children, and the nature of the education provided to the children.

⌐ CLASS STRUGGLE 101 ⌐

Barbara Ehrenreich

In this article, the author toys with a number of college
courses. She turns the mirror of the university toward itself
and examines social inequality within its academic walls.
How might a course look that compares the luxuries of the
campus alumni dwellings with the trailer park for the campus
food-service workers? She cites specific examples of strikes at
major universities around the United States, including Harvard, Miami, North Carolina, and Yale, where students and
faculty are activists on behalf of campus workers.

O n the evening of August 24, I had dinner with Randy Marcum, who works in the boiler room at Miami University of
Ohio. Joining us were about ten other campus workers, plus
some of their student supporters. It was a hefty meal—the best the
Holiday Inn had to offer—complete with wine and dessert. Which
was a good thing, because three weeks later, Marcum was on a hunger
strike to dramatize the poverty of Miami University's food service and
maintenance workers.

Welcome to higher education, twenty-first-century style, where
the most important course offered is not listed in the college catalog.
It's called Class Struggle, and it pits the men in suits—administrators
and trustees—against the men and women who keep the school running: maintenance workers, groundspeople, clerical and technical
workers, housekeepers, food service workers. Yale has gotten all the
national attention, with its tumultuous three-week-long strike that
just ended in a stunning victory for the university's clerical and maintenance workers. But similar clashes are going on in less illustrious
places, like the University of North Carolina at Chapel Hill, where
housekeepers, who have been trying to win union recognition for
years, led a lively rally and teach-in on September 23.

Reprinted from the *Progressive*, November 2003.

As for Miami University, 460 maintenance workers are now out on strike, as I write at the end of September. Randy has ended his fast in order to build up energy for the picket line. The students have erected a tent city in front of the administration building. And faculty members are planning their own night in the tent city. Union picketers humiliated the university by turning away the union camera crews who had come to televise a Miami RedHawks vs. Cincinnati Bearcats game.

College presidents, deans, provosts, chancellors—along with their deputies, assistants, and other members of the ever-proliferating educational administrative workforce—insist that their labor problems are a sorry distraction from their institutions' noble purpose of enlightening young minds. But administrators like to cloak themselves in the moral authority of Western Civilization, such as it is, which means that labor issues are hardly peripheral to the university's educational mission. On an increasing number of campuses, incoming students are greeted at a formal fall convocation in which the top administrators—suited up in full medieval mortarboard-and-gown attire—deliver platitudinous speeches about Character, Integrity, and Truth. The message is that these weirdly costumed folks are not mere executives of a corporation but the guardians of an ancient and sacred tradition. So when these same dignitaries turn out to be grossly underpaying their employees and harassing the "troublemakers" among them, they do so with the apparent blessing of Aristotle, Plato, and Shakespeare.

If the university has so much to teach about social inequality, why shouldn't the students get credit for learning it? The covert lessons from the administration should be formalized as course offerings. Here's the curriculum.

Elementary Class Structure of the United States: The University as Microcosm. In this four-credit course, we will examine the pay gradient from housekeeper (approximately $19,000/year) to president (more than $270,000 for Miami University's James C. Garland and about $500,000 for Yale's Richard Levin). In the final exam, students will be asked to discuss the rationale for this pay gap in terms of the payees' contributions to the university, ongoing housing and wardrobe expenses, and intrinsic human worth.

Presidential Architecture: A three-credit seminar course featuring field trips through university-provided presidential dwellings, including "great rooms," wet bars, saunas, guest suites, and exercise rooms, with a side trip, if time permits, to the trailer parks favored by the housekeeping and maintenance staff.

Race, Gender, and Occupational Preference: In this advanced sociology seminar, we will analyze the way campus workers sort themselves into various occupations on the basis of race and gender, and we will explore various theories attempting to explain this phenomenon—for example, the Innate Athleticism theory of why African Americans so often prefer manual labor, and the Nimble Fingers theory of why females can usually be found doing the clerical work.

Topics in University Financing: A four-credit business course tracing the development of the current two-pronged approach to financing institutions of higher learning—tuition increases for the students plus pay decreases for the staff. Alternative approaches to financing, featuring militant campaigns for adequate public funding for higher education, will be thoroughly critiqued.

A cynic might say that the true purpose of college is to teach exactly such lessons. After all, college graduates are a relative elite, comprising only 25 percent of the adult population, and they are expected to fill the kind of administrative and managerial jobs that make it a positive advantage to be able to starve workers, impose layoffs, and bust unions without losing a minute of sleep. Some students catch on with lightning-like speed, such as Yale's precocious Scott Wexler, eighteen, who confided to *The New York Times,* "I kind of like walking through the picket lines." This young man will make a fine assistant regional manager at Wal-Mart—or possibly a college president.

Fortunately, not all students are buying the administrations' lesson plan. At Harvard in the spring of 2001, students occupied an administration building for twenty-one days to persuade the administration to bargain with campus janitors, many of whom were paid only $6.50 an hour. Last spring, Stanford students went on their own hunger strike in support of campus blue collar workers. And it's not just the super-elite schools that have been generating vigorous student-labor alliances. At mainstream public universities like those of Maryland and Virginia, there are plenty of students who would agree with Miami University's Justin Katko, when he writes that he got involved in the campus workers' struggle because "I could not allow such extreme disparities as are found on college campuses . . . to exist without being ashamed of myself for apathy."

It's hard to concentrate in classrooms that were cleaned during the night by people who can barely make rent. You tend to choke on your chicken fingers when the cafeteria is staffed by men and women who have to work a second job in order to feed their own children.

Questions

1. Discuss student activism at your college or university. Is there student apathy?

2. Investigate the salaries of employees at your campus. Be sure and locate a range of salaries. Do service workers make a living wage based on the cost of living in the local communities?

3. Apply Marx's labor theory of value to compare and contrast the work of university administrators and university staff workers.

4. Using Ehrenreich's four courses as models, recommend a new course to the chairperson of your major department that applies social inequality to the infrastructure and workers at your university.

SILENCE IS NOT WITHOUT VOICE: INCLUDING DEAF CULTURE WITHIN MULTICULTURAL CURRICULA

H. Dirksen
L. Bauman
Jennifer Drake

A movement to recognize American Sign Language as a valid language (including by colleges and universities as a language that would fulfill their foreign language requirement) began in the 1980s. Research shows that ASL meets all of the requirements of being a recognized language, including the fact that it has a grammar (a set of rules governing it) and is shared by a community. The community that shares this language still struggles for recognition as a distinct culture. This issue is complicated by the fact that not all deaf people identify as Deaf (the capital "D" is used to identify the Deaf culture and individuals who identify as members of it). In this article from Radical Teacher, Bauman and Drake make a case for using a Deafness as culture model rather than the deafness as disability model, when incorporating the topic into multicultural curricula.

At a time when universities work to incorporate multicultural curricula and canon revisions, they still perpetuate the pathologization of Deaf culture, language, and literature.[1] Most universities have yet to realize that Deaf people are not a loosely knit group of audiologically

---

Reprinted from *Radical Teacher*, fall 1995.

impaired individuals, but are, rather, a linguistic and cultural minority whose complex history, language, and literature warrant sustained recognition. Only a handful of American universities, for example, presently accept American Sign Language for legitimate language credit. As social science and humanities departments do not perceive Deaf studies to fall within their curricular domain, the study of "deafness" becomes relegated to special education departments—discursive straightjackets that confine Deaf culture to pathological constructions.

But what can a predominantly "hearing" university without a Deaf studies department do to rewrite these misunderstandings about the Deaf community? This is a question that we have been asking for different reasons and from different positions. When Dirkson crossed the border into a Deaf cultural space as a dormitory supervisor at the Colorado School for the Deaf and the Blind, he began to redefine his own pathological notions about Deaf persons. The Deaf students and faculty were not isolated and linguistically deprived as he had assumed; rather, they enjoyed a strong sense of community based on an "official" language. He, not the Deaf, became the linguistic outsider. Upon returning to a university setting, Dirksen found that even "progressive" language and literature faculty did not recognize American Sign Language as an "official" language or Deaf identity as a cultural identity.

Over the past few summers Jennifer had been creating the curriculum for "Narratives of Struggle," a writing course exploring the centrality of so-called marginal communities in forging American (multi)culture. When Dirksen became co-instructor for the course, the personal and pedagogical benefits of linking Jennifer's work in multicultural studies with Dirksen's work on Deaf culture became obvious. We hoped that the multicultural context of the course would encourage an engaged reading of Deafness as culture rather than deafness as disability, and that the texts on deafness as disability, and that the texts on Deaf studies would disrupt hearing teachers' and students' reductive ways of thinking about culture, identity, and community.

We taught "Narratives of Struggle" as part of the 1994 Binghamton Enrichment Program (BEP) at SUNY's Binghamton University. BEP is part of New York State's Educational Opportunity Program (EOP) at Binghamton, which provides academic support to students from educationally and economically disadvantaged backgrounds. As such, students in the Binghamton Enrichment Program come from the working class or working poor; some come from group homes or foster care; many grew up in single-parent families; most are from New York City, though a few live upstate; and the majority are of African, Caribbean, Latino, and/or Asian descent.

Students enrolled in "Narratives of Struggle" also enrolled in "Media (Ill) Literacy and Self-Governance," taught by Kassie Fleisher. While the media studies course taught students to read the media's representations of "truth" in critical and complex ways, our writing course looked at texts that bell hooks would call "critical fixtures"— texts that resist dominant discourses, challenge our expectations of what "literature" is/does, and require the development of engaged reading strategies. Hooks's essay "Narratives of Struggle," in Philomena Mariani's Critical Fictions: *The Politics of Imaginative Writing*, served as the template for the course, providing students with a critical vocabulary—"(de)colonization," "political self-recovery," "resistance," "imagination"—that they could use, and struggle with, throughout the course.

Each week had its own thematic focus, such as "Resisting Silences/Finding Voices," "Hybridity and Cultural Survival," and "(De)Colonization, Coalition Building, and Difference." At the start of each week the class wrestled with the meanings and implications of these titles by brainstorming associations on the chalkboard, unpacking dictionary definitions, returning to hooks's essay, an playing with the critical possibilities suggested by these title phrases.

Discussions of Deaf culture first occurred directly after reading Maxine Hong Kingston's "Song for a Barbarian Reed Pipe" during the "Resisting Silences/Finding Voices" week. This juxtaposition of texts and cultures worked to extend and to complicate the discussions of language and (multi)cultural identity, voice, and silence that we had begun in response to Kingston's work. Student facilitator Vivian Lei began a lively discussion about whether or not silences can work as a strategy of resistance and about how one person's silence is another person's expressiveness—think of Kingston's black paintings "full of possibility," about to reveal "mighty operas." Faced with the difference between Kingston's empowering reading of her own paintings and her teacher's pathologization of them, students began to talk about negotiating two or more languages and culture. While some students focused on their own and Kingston's struggles to live "inbetween" and the pressure to assimilate, others described the benefits of drawing on two languages and cultural traditions, pointing out that "inbetween-ness" might be lived not as culture clash but as a powerful position from which to speak and construct personal and community identities.

These conversations about language, culture, assimilation, and re-sistance provided a strong transition into discussions of Deaf culture as represented in Mark Medoff's play *Children of a Lesser God* and ex-cerpts from Bernard Bragg's *Lessons in Laughter: The Autobiography of a Deaf Actor,* as signed to Eugene Bergman. Bragg's autobiography raises issues of the role of education as a means to coerce assimilation into "hearing" culture. Student facilitators Silvia Sanchez and Sabrina Lebron led the class through a close reading of Bragg's title scene in which a hearing teacher forces his Deaf students to laugh like "hu-mans," that is, hearing people. Students were appalled that hearing culture could be so coercive and violent in the name of education.

We then moved on to Medoff's play, which also takes up the role of education in disciplining "cultural subjects." In addition, since Medoff is a hearing playwright, the play opens up discussion about "hearing" representations of Deaf persons. These issues of representation become especially pronounced when the written text of the play is juxtaposed with the film version. Silvia and Sabrina, for ex-ample, brought in film clips in order to illustrate the film's depoliti-cization of Deafness in favor of the love story, which, they agreed, was more likely to sell movie tickets. Reading and watching these two tex-tual representations of Deafness as imagined by hearing people en-couraged the class to reflect upon our own situation as a hearing classroom talking about Deaf culture. In this situation, hearing stu-dents and teachers might think of themselves not as speaking in place of Deaf people—for Deaf people may "speak" through texts and in-vited lecturers and performers—but rather, as hearing people engage in self-reflective conversation about the audist oppression of the Deaf community.

Student Youlla Pierre chose to write one of her papers about *Chil-dren of a Lesser God* in order to explore more fully dominant cultural assumptions about the Deaf community. In the following passage, she articulates the differences between "hearing" and "listening," "silence" and "deafness:"

Hearing is when you have heard what a person has said and you learn and empathize with that person. . . . Deaf means that due to biological reasons you were born without the ability to hear voices. It could also mean that you are unwilling to hear. The word silence means not speaking with your voice or it could also mean that you, unwillingly or willingly, want to communicate using other methods . . . [The Deaf] have the knowledge to communicate in other ways . . . that may not be known to us . . . Maybe that makes us hearing people the silent ones to them.

Youlla went on to illustrate her ideas by writing about two major characters in the play: Sarah is a strong Deaf woman and James, Sarah's hearing husband and a teacher at the school for the Deaf, tries to teach Sarah to speak. Drawing on Friere's discussion of the "deposits" made in banking education and hooks's discussion of colonized minds, Youlla writes:

James had a colonized mind . . . James became fearful of Sarah's independence because what would society think of a person who cannot overpower or as they would put it nicely, "help" a "disabled" person? . . . And since society had thrust upon him the idea that he had to take care of her . . . he thought that society would think less of him because he would not be able to control his "disabled" child. So because of that feeling, James ended up turning a "deaf" ear to Sarah . . . He only thought of himself and his need for her to [talk]. He did not leave himself any room to empathize with Sarah at all.

In her paper, Youlla continued to connect the inability to "hear" with the inability to listen and to empathize in order to argue that the dominant culture is "disabled" by its inability to listen to the "voices" of different communities. By creating the distinction between biological and empathetic deafness, Youlla articulated a convincing argument for depathologizing Deaf identity.

Clearly, discussing Deaf language and culture in a multicultural context encouraged students to consider that American Sign Language is a "real" language and that the Deaf are a "real" cultural community. For example, a paper by Amoy Chambers argued that bell hooks's call for "political self-recovery" requires the use of so-called "minority" languages like American Sign Language. Reading a scene from the film in which Sarah starts dancing with James but ends up dancing with herself and loving it, Amoy suggests that Sarah resists the label "disabled" by claiming an identity based on the powerful expressiveness of her body's movements in dance and sign. Amoy also links the political and cultural struggles of the Deaf community to other resistance movements:

> If sign language is a recognized language, then why is it not implemented in our curriculum as other languages are? So, society is overtly disregarding another culture, as it always does . . . society is not willing to acknowledge subjects/people that are different.

As the course continued, this acknowledgement of Deaf persons as cultural subjects dovetailed with discussions about identity-formation within multiple communities, including educational institutions such as the classroom and the university where our discussions were taking place. Students began to see that the family is not the only site for the transmission of cultural identity and that communities include, and are built from, our differences and multiple allegiances.

Including texts about Deaf culture in a multicultural curriculum demonstrated to students that "culture" cannot be thought of monolithically only in terms of "race." This realization opened the way for strong discussions of essays by Gloria Anzaldúa and Audre Lorde, in which the writers resist bearing allegiance to one community/self at the expense of another. In fact, students began to think about Anzaldúa's and Lorde's lesbianism in terms of "culture" and "community" and so, congruent with our discussions of Deaf culture, began to move away from a reductive pathologization of homosexuality. In later weeks, students continued to talk about the Deaf, gays, lesbians, and virtually all American cultures and subjectivities as hybrid, multicultural identities and so began to link various resistance struggles to their own struggles against racism and classism.

When approached with critical awareness, incorporating Deaf culture into multicultural curricula can bear substantial rewards for both Deaf and hearing communities. For the Deaf, recontextualizing Deaf identity in a cultural framework alongside Latinos, African-Americans, Chinese-Americans, gays and lesbians, and other cultural/racial/ethnic groups represents significant advancement toward the recognition that the Deaf community is a linguistic minority in the United States. In addition, hearing students introduced to the relevant historical, political, and social issues surrounding Deaf culture are encouraged to expand and to challenge their existing notions of multiculturalism, disability, and language. Such expansion of terms becomes a useful means of developing a wider, more inclusive critical consciousness among students and teachers whose notions of multiculturalism tend to over-determine race at the expense of other significant and simultaneous sites of difference. Such reciprocal benefits to the Deaf and hearing communities serve to emancipate both from oppressive misconceptions about disability, language, and cultural identity.

Endnote

[1]We use "Deaf," rather than "deaf," in order to distinguish between Deaf people who identify with Deaf culture and deaf people who do not. This distinction also helps to clarify the differences between Deaf education (bilingual/bicultural education) and deaf education (the historically hearing-dominated forms of education based on the medical view of deafness).

Questions

1. What does it mean to understand "Deafness as culture rather than deafness as disability"? Why do people tend to see deafness as a disability?

2. Explain the meaning of "Silence is not without voice" with respect to Deaf culture.

3. Delineate Bauman and Drake's case for including Deafness in multicultural curricula.

4. How has "hearing" society oppressed Deaf (and deaf) people?

5. How is "audist" oppression similar to and different from race, sex, or class discrimination?

❧ BLACK MEN ❧
AND PUBLIC SPACE

Brent Staples

Brent Staples (1951–) was born in Chester, Pennsylvania. He received his B. A. in behavioral sciences from Widener University in Chester and then his Ph.D. in psychology from the University of Chicago. He has worked as a writer for the Chicago Sun-Times, Chicago *magazine, and* Down Beat *magazine. He has written also for* New York Times Magazine, Ms., *and* Harper's. *Staples joined the editorial board of the* New York Times, *where he writes regularly on culture and politics. The following essay was first published in* Ms. *in 1986 and then in the revised version printed here in* Harper's *in 1987. In it Staples provides insight into a contemporary social phenomenon resulting from the racism and violence common in our world.*

1   My first victim was a woman—white, well dressed, probably in her late twenties. I came upon her late one evening on a deserted street in Hyde Park, a relatively affluent neighborhood in an otherwise mean, impoverished section of Chicago. As I swung onto the avenue behind her, there seemed to be a discreet, uninflammatory distance between us. Not so. She cast back a worried glance. To her, the youngish black man—a broad six feet two inches with a beard and billowing hair, both hands shoved into the pockets of a bulky military jacket—seemed menacingly close. After a few more quick glimpses, she picked up her pace and was soon running in earnest. Within seconds she disappeared into a cross street.

That was more than a decade ago. I was twenty-two years old, a graduate student newly arrived at the University of Chicago. It was in the echo of that terrified woman's footfalls that I first began to know the unwieldy inheritance I'd come into—the ability to alter public space in ugly ways. It was clear that she thought herself the quarry of a mugger, a rapist, or worse. Suffering a bout of insomnia, however, I was stalking sleep, not defenseless wayfarers. As a softy who is scarcely able to take a knife to a raw chicken—let alone hold one to a person's throat—I was surprised, embarrassed, and dismayed all at once. Her flight made me feel like an accomplice in tyranny. It also made it clear that I was indistinguishable from the muggers who occasionally seeped into the area from the surrounding ghetto. That first encounter, and those that followed, signified that a vast, unnerving gulf lay between nighttime pedestrians—particularly women—and me. And I soon gathered that being perceived as dangerous is a hazard in itself. I only needed to turn a corner into a dicey situation, or crowd some frightened, armed person in a foyer somewhere, or make an errant move after being pulled over by a policeman. Where fear and weapons meet—and they often do in urban America—there is always the possibility of death.

In that first year, my first away from my hometown, I was to become thoroughly familiar with the language of fear. At dark, shadowy intersections, I could cross in front of a car stopped at a traffic light and elicit the *thunk, thunk, thunk, thunk* of the driver—black, white, male, or female—hammering down the door locks. On less traveled streets after dark, I grew accustomed to but never comfortable with people crossing to the other side of the street rather than pass me. Then there were the standard unpleasantries with policemen, doormen, bouncers, cabdrivers, and others whose business it is to screen out troublesome individuals *before* there is any nastiness.

I moved to New York nearly two years ago and I have remained an avid night walker. In central Manhattan, the near constant crowd cover minimizes tense one-on-one street encounters. Elsewhere—in SoHo, for example, where sidewalks are narrow and tightly spaced buildings shut out the sky—things can get very taut indeed.

After dark, on the warrenlike streets of Brooklyn where I live, I often see women who fear the worst from me. They seem to have set their faces on neutral, and with their purse straps strung across their chests bandolier-style, they forge ahead as though bracing themselves against being tackled. I understand, of course, that the danger they perceive is not a hallucination. Women are particularly vulnerable to street violence, and young black males are drastically overrepresented among the perpetrators of that violence. Yet these truths are no solace against the kind of alienation that comes of being ever the suspect, a fearsome entity with whom pedestrians avoid making eye contact.

It is not altogether clear to me how I reached the ripe old age of twenty-two without being conscious of the lethality nighttime pedestrians attributed to me. Perhaps it was because in Chester, Pennsylvania, the small, angry industrial town where I came of age in the 1960s, I was scarcely noticeable against a backdrop of gang warfare, street knifings, and murders. I grew up one of the good boys, had perhaps a half-dozen fistfights. In retrospect, my shyness of combat has clear sources.

As a boy, I saw countless tough guys locked away; I have since buried several, too. They were babies, really—a teenage cousin, a brother of twenty-two, a childhood friend in his mid-twenties—all gone down in episodes of bravado played out in the streets. I came to doubt the virtues of intimidation early on. I chose, perhaps unconsciously, to remain a shadow—timid, but a survivor.

The fearsomeness mistakenly attributed to me in public places often has a perilous flavor. The most frightening of these confusions occurred in the late 1970s and early 1980s, when I worked as a journalist in Chicago. One day, rushing into the office of a magazine I was writing for with a deadline story in hand, I was mistaken for a burglar. The office manager called security and, with an ad hoc posse, pursued me through the labyrinthine halls, nearly to my editor's door. I had no way of proving who I was. I could only move briskly toward the company of someone who knew me.

Another time I was on assignment for a local paper and killing time before an interview. I entered a jewelry store on the city's affluent Near North Side. The proprietor excused herself and returned with an enormous red Doberman pinscher straining at the end of a leash. She stood, the dog extended toward me, silent to my questions, her eyes bulging nearly out of her head. I took a cursory look around, nodded, and bade her good night.

10 Relatively speaking, however, I never fared as badly as another 10
black male journalist. He went to nearby Waukegan, Illinois, a couple of summers ago to work on a story about a murderer who was born

there. Mistaking the reporter for the killer, police officers hauled him from his car at gunpoint and but for his press credentials would probably have tried to book him. Such episodes are not uncommon. Black men trade tales like this all the time.

Over the years, I learned to smother the rage I felt at so often being taken for a criminal. Not to do so would surely have led to madness. I now take precautions to make myself less threatening. I move about with care, particularly late in the evening. I give a wide berth to nervous people on subway platforms during the wee hours, particularly when I have exchanged business clothes for jeans. If I happen to be entering a building behind some people who appear skittish, I may walk by, letting them clear the lobby before I return, so as not to seem to be following them. I have been calm and extremely congenial on those rare occasions when I've been pulled over by the police.

And on late-evening constitutionals I employ what has proved to be an excellent tension-reducing measure: I whistle melodies from Beethoven and Vivaldi and the more popular classical composers. Even steely New Yorkers hunching toward nighttime destinations seem to relax, and occasionally they even join in the tune. Virtually everybody seems to sense that a mugger wouldn't be warbling bright, sunny selections from Vivaldi's *Four Seasons*. It is my equivalent of the cowbell that hikers wear when they know they are in bear country.

Questions on Meaning

1. Does Staples blame the people who fear him on the street at night? Does he explain the source of the societal problem he describes?

2. Staples says he has "learned to smother the rage I felt at so often being taken for a criminal"—but clearly he has not forgotten his pain and anger. How would you describe his attitude now toward this reality in our society?

3. In addition to being black and male, what about Staples might lead to some people feeling afraid to have him walking behind them on a quiet street at night? To what extent does Staples discuss these other factors? To what extent do you feel some women might react similarly to a large white man dressed in a military jacket walking behind them on a quiet street at night? Comment on what is different, however, about being black in this circumstance.

Questions on Rhetorical Strategy and Style

1. Much of the power of this essay comes from the many examples Staples gives of the phenomenon he is writing about. Choose two examples of how his presence affected others in public space and analyze them phrase by phrase, image by image, to see how his writing has this impact.

2. Analyze Staples' style. Pay attention to both the colloquial, conversational language of phrases such as "a dicey situation" and the more formal language of his sociological observations. Make a list of words that describe his style.

Writing Assignments

1. Most of us, male or female, black or white, have been in situations in which we felt like Staples' "victim"—in the presence of someone we interpreted as a threat to our well-being. Looking back at such situations and fears, after having read this essay, do you now think you were justified in your fear? Would you now wonder, in the same circumstances, whether you might be offending the person by reacting with fear? Or, not knowing anything more about the person, are you still in a better position reacting as if the person *is* a threat? What do you think Staples would advise you to do in such a situation?

2. It has been said that it is natural to fear the unknown. Do you see this as a clear cause-effect relationship? Think of circumstances in which you would fear something or someone unknown. Try to define the characteristics that would lead to fear. Then write an essay in which you explain your thoughts on the relationship between the unknown and fear.

❧ ON BEING A CRIPPLE ❧

Nancy Mairs

Nancy Mairs (1943–) was born in California, attended college in New England, and now lives in Tucson, Arizona. She earned her M. F. A. in creative writing and Ph.D. in literature from the University of Arizona and has taught writing and worked as an editor for many years. She has written a book of poetry, In All the Rooms of the Yellow House *(1984), and a number of collections of essays and autobiographical sketches, including* i*(1986),* Remembering the Bone House *(1989),* Carnal Acts *(1990),* Ordinary Time *(1993),* Voice Lessons *(1994),* Waist-High in the World: A Life Among the Nondisabled *(1996), and* A Troubled Guest: Life and Death Stories *(2001). As you'll see in the first few sentences of the following autobiographical essay, published in 1993, Mairs writes with an honest, outspoken style that immediately engages you in her subject.*

> *To escape is nothing. Not to escape is nothing.*
> —Louise Bogan

1   The other day I was thinking of writing an essay on being a cripple. I was thinking hard in one of the stalls of the women's room in my office building, as I was shoving my shirt into my jeans and tugging up my zipper. Preoccupied, I flushed, picked up my book bag, took my cane down from the hook, and unlatched the door. So many movements unbalanced me, and as I pulled the door open I fell over backward, landing fully clothed on the toilet seat with my legs splayed in front me: the old beetle-on-its-back routine. Saturday afternoon, the building deserted, I was free to laugh aloud as I wriggled back to my feet, my voice bouncing off the yellowish tiles from all

From *Plaintext*. Published by The University of Arizona Press. Copyright © 1986 by Nancy Mairs.

directions. Had anyone been there with me, I'd have been still and faint and hot with chagrin. I decided that it was high time to write the essay.

First, the matter of semantics. I am a cripple. I choose this word to name me. I choose from among several possibilities, the most common of which are "handicapped" and "disabled." I made the choice a number of years ago, without thinking, unaware of my motives for doing so. Even now, I'm not sure what those motives are, but I recognize that they are complex and not entirely flattering. People—crippled or not—wince at the word "cripple," as they do not at "handicapped" or "disabled." Perhaps I want them to wince. I want them to see me as a tough customer, one to whom the fates/gods/viruses have not been kind, but who can face the brutal truth of her existence squarely. As a cripple, I swagger.

But, to be fair to myself, a certain amount of honesty underlies my choice. "Cripple" seems to me a clean word, straightforward and precise. It has an honorable history, having made its first appearance in the Lindisfarne Gospel in the tenth century. As a lover of words, I like the accuracy with which it describes my condition: I have lost the full use of my limbs. "Disabled," by contrast, suggests an incapacity, physical or mental. And I certainly don't like "handicapped," which implies that I have deliberately been put at a disadvantage, by whom I can't imagine (my God is not a Handicapper General), in order to equalize chances in the great race of life. These words seem to me to be moving away from my condition, to be widening the gap between word and reality. Most remote is the recently coined euphemism "differently abled," which partakes of the same semantic hopefulness that transformed countries from "undeveloped" to "underdeveloped," then to "less developed," and finally to "developing" nations. People have continued to starve in those countries during the shift. Some realities do not obey the dictates of language.

Mine is one of them. Whatever you call me, I remain crippled. But I don't care what you call me, so long as it isn't "differently abled," which strikes me as pure verbal garbage designed, by its ability to describe anyone, to describe no one. I subscribe to George Orwell's thesis that "the slovenliness of our language makes it easier for us to have foolish thoughts." And I refuse to participate in the degeneration of the language to the extent that I deny that I have lost anything in the course of this calamitous disease; I refuse to pretend that the only differences between you and me are the various ordinary ones that distinguish any one person from another. But call me "disabled" or "handicapped" if you like. I have long since grown accustomed to them; and if they are vague, at least they hint at the truth. Moreover, I use them myself. Society is no readier to accept crippledness than to accept death, war, sex, sweat, or wrinkles. I would never refer to another person as a cripple. It is the word I use to name only myself.

5   I haven't always been crippled, a fact for which I am soundly grateful. To be whole of limb is, I know from experience, infinitely more pleasant and useful than to be crippled; and if that knowledge leaves me open to bitterness at my loss, the physical soundness I once enjoyed (though I did not enjoy it half enough) is well worth the occasional stab of regret. Though never any good at sports, I was a normally active child and young adult. I climbed trees, played hopscotch, jumped rope, skated, swam, rode my bicycle, sailed. I despised team sports, spending some of the wretchedest afternoons of my life sweaty and humiliated, behind a field-hockey stick and under a basketball hoop. I tramped alone for miles along the bridle paths that webbed the woods behind the house I grew up in. I swayed through countless dim hours in the arms of one man or another under the scattered shot of light from mirrored balls, and gyrated through countless more as Tab Hunter and Johnny Mathis gave way to the Rolling Stones, Creedence Clearwater Revival, Cream. I walked down the aisle. I pushed baby carriages, changed tires in the rain, marched for peace.

When I was twenty-eight I started to trip and drop things. What at first seemed my natural clumsiness soon became too pronounced to shrug off. I consulted a neurologist, who told me that I had a brain tumor. A battery of tests, increasingly disagreeable, revealed no tumor. About a year and a half later I developed a blurred spot in one eye. I had, at last, the episodes "disseminated in space and time" requisite for a diagnosis: multiple sclerosis. I have never been sorry for the doctor's initial misdiagnosis, however. For almost a week, until the negative results of the tests were in, I thought that I was going to die right away. Every day for the past nearly ten years, then, has been a kind of gift. I accept all gifts.

Multiple sclerosis is a chronic degenerative disease of the central nervous system, in which the myelin that sheathes the nerves is somehow eaten away and scar tissue forms in its place, interrupting the nerves' signals. During its course, which is unpredictable and uncontrollable, one may lose vision, hearing, speech, the ability to walk, control of bladder and/or bowels, strength in any or all extremities, sensitivity to touch, vibration, and/or pain, potency, coordination of movements—the list of possibilities is lengthy and yes, horrifying. One may also lose one's sense of humor. That's the easiest to lose and the hardest to survive without.

In the past ten years, I have sustained some of these losses. Characteristic of MS are sudden attacks, called exacerbations, followed by remissions, and these I have not had. Instead, my disease has been slowly progressive. My left leg is now so weak that I walk with the aid of a brace and a cane; and for distances I use an Amigo, a variation on the electric wheelchair that looks rather like an electrified kiddie car. I no longer have much use of my left hand. Now my right side is weakening as well. I still have the blurred spot in my right eye. Overall, though, I've been lucky so far. My world has, of necessity, been circumscribed by my losses, but the terrain left me has been ample enough for me to continue many of the activities that absorb me: writing, teaching, raising children and cats and plants and snakes, reading, speaking publicly about MS and depression, even playing bridge with people patient and honorable enough to let me scatter cards every which way without sneaking a peek.

Lest I begin to sound like Pollyanna, however, let me say that I don't like having MS. I hate it. My life holds realities—harsh ones, some of them—that no right-minded human being ought to accept without grumbling. One of them is fatigue. I know of no one with MS who does not complain of bone-weariness; in a disease that presents an astonishing variety of symptoms, fatigue seems to be a common factor. I wake up in the morning feeling the way most people do at the end of a bad day, and I take it from there. As a result, I spend a lot of time *in extremis* and, impatient with limitation, I tend to ignore my fatigue until my body breaks down in some way and forces rest. Then I miss picnics, dinner parties, poetry readings, the brief visits of old friends from out of town. The offspring of a puritanical tradition of exceptional venerability, I cannot view these lapses without shame. My life often seems a series of small failures to do as I ought.

I lead, on the whole, an ordinary life, probably rather like the one I would have led had I not had MS. I am lucky that my predilections were already solitary, sedentary, and bookish—unlike the world-famous French cellist I have read about, or the young woman I talked with one long afternoon who wanted only to be a jockey. I had just begun graduate school when I found out something was wrong with me, and I have remained, interminably, a graduate student. Perhaps I would not have if I'd thought I had the stamina to return to a full-time job as a technical editor; but I've enjoyed my studies.

In addition to studying, I teach writing courses. I also teach medical students how to give neurological examinations. I pick up freelance editing jobs here and there. I have raised a foster son and sent him into the world, where he has made me two grandbabies, and I am still escorting my daughter and son through adolescence. I go to Mass every Saturday. I am a superb, if messy, cook. I am also an enthusiastic laundress, capable of sorting a hamper full of clothes into five subtly differentiated piles, but a terrible housekeeper. I can do italic writing and, in an emergency, bathe an oil-soaked cat. I play a fiendish game of Scrabble. When I have the time and the money, I like to sit on my front steps with my husband, drinking Amaretto and smoking a cigar, as we imagine our counterparts in Leningrad and make sure that the sun gets down once more behind the sharp childish scrawl of the Tucson Mountains.

This lively plenty has its bleak complement, of course, in all the things I can no longer do. I will never run again, except in dreams, and one day I may have to write that I will never walk again. I like to go camping, but I can't follow George and the children along the trails that wander out of a campsite through the desert or into the mountains. In fact, even on the level I've learned never to check the weather or try to hold a coherent conversation: I need all my attention for my wayward feet. Of late, I have begun to catch myself wondering how people can propel themselves without canes. With only one usable hand, I have to select my clothing with care not so much for style as for ease of ingress and egress, and even so, dressing can be laborious. I can no longer do fine stitchery, pick up babies, play the piano, braid my hair. I am immobilized by acute attacks of depression, which may or may not be physiologically related to MS but are certainly its logical concomitant.

These two elements, the plenty and the privation, are never pure, nor are the delight and wretchedness that accompany them. Almost every pickle that I get into as a result of my weakness and clumsiness—and I get into plenty—is funny as well as maddening and sometimes painful. I recall one May afternoon when a friend and I were going out for a drink after finishing up at school. As we were climbing into opposite sides of my car, chatting, I tripped and fell, flat and hard, onto the asphalt parking lot, my abrupt departure interrupting him in mid-sentence. "Where'd you go?" he called as he came around the back of the car to find me hauling myself up by the door frame. "Are you all right?" Yes, I told him, I was fine, just a bit rattly, and we drove off to find a shady patio and some beer. When I got home an hour or so later, my daughter greeted me with "What have you done to yourself?" I looked down. One elbow of my white turtleneck with the green froggies, one knee of my white trousers, one white kneesock were blood-soaked. We peeled off the clothes and inspected the damage, which was nasty enough but not alarming. That part wasn't funny: The abrasions took a long time to heal, and one got a little infected. Even so, when I think of my friend talking earnestly, suddenly, to the hot thin air while I dropped from his view as though through a trap door, I find the image as silly as something from a Marx Brothers movie.

I may find it easier than other cripples to amuse myself because I live propped by the acceptance and the assistance and, sometimes, the amusement of those around me. Grocery clerks tear my checks out of my checkbook for me, and sales clerks find chairs to put into dressing rooms when I want to try on clothes. The people I work with make sure I teach at times when I am least likely to be fatigued, in places I can get to, with the materials I need. My students, with one anonymous exception (in an end-of-the-semester evaluation) have been unperturbed by my disability. Some even like it. One was immensely cheered by the information that I paint my own fingernails; she decided, she told me, that if I could go to such trouble over fine details, she could keep on writing essays. I suppose I became some sort of bright-fingered muse. She wrote good essays, too.

15   The most important struts in the framework of my existence, of   15 course, are my husband and children. Dismayingly few marriages survive the MS test, and why should they? Most twenty-two- and nineteen-year-olds, like George and me, can vow in clear conscience, after a childhood of chickenpox and summer colds, to keep one another in sickness and in health so long as they both shall live. Not many are equipped for catastrophe: the dismay, the depression, the extra work, the boredom that a degenerative disease can insinuate into a relationship. And our society, with its emphasis on fun and its association of fun with physical performance, offers little encouragement for a whole spouse to stay with a crippled partner. Children experience similar stresses when faced with a crippled parent, and they are more helpless, since parents and children can't usually get divorced. They hate, of

course, to be different from their peers, and the child whose mother is tacking down the aisle of a school auditorium packed with proud parents like a Cape Cod dinghy in a stiff breeze jolly well stands out in a crowd. Deprived of legal divorce, the child can at least deny the mother's disability, even her existence, forgetting to tell her about recitals and PTA meetings, refusing to accompany her to stores or church or the movies, never inviting friends to the house. Many do.

But I've been limping along for ten years now, and so far George and the children are still at my left elbow, holding tight. Anne and Matthew vacuum floors and dust furniture and haul trash and rake up dog droppings and button my cuffs and bake lasagne and Toll House cookies with just enough grumbling so I know that they don't have brain fever. And far from hiding me, they're forever dragging me by racks of fancy clothes or through teeming school corridors, or welcoming gaggles of friends while I'm wandering through the house in Anne's filmy pink babydoll pajamas. George generally calls before he brings someone home, but he does just as many dumb thankless chores as the children. And they all yell at me, laugh at some of my jokes, write me funny letters when we're apart—in short, treat me as an ordinary human being for whom they have some use. I think they like me. Unless they're faking. . . .

Faking. There's the rub. Tugging at the fringes of my consciousness always is the terror that people are kind to me only because I'm a cripple. My mother almost shattered me once, with that instinct mothers have—blind, I think, in this case, but unerring nonetheless—for striking blows along the fault-lines of their children's hearts, by telling me, in an attack on my selfishness, "We all have to make allowances for you, of course, because of the way you are." From the distance of a couple of years, I have to admit that I haven't any idea just what she meant, and I'm not sure that she knew either. She was awfully angry. But at the time, as the words thudded home, I felt my worst fear, suddenly realized. I could bear being called selfish: I am. But I couldn't bear the corroboration that those around me were doing in fact what I'd always suspected them of doing, professing fondness while silently putting up with me because of the way I am. A cripple. I've been a little cracked ever since.

Along with this fear that people are secretly accepting shoddy goods comes a relentless pressure to please—to prove myself worth the burdens I impose, I guess, or to build a substantial account of goodwill against which I may write drafts in times of need. Part of the pressure arises from social expectations. In our society, anyone who deviates from the norm had better find some way to compensate. Like fat people, who are expected to be jolly, cripples must bear their lot meekly and cheerfully. A grumpy cripple isn't playing by the rules. And much of the pressure is self-generated. Early on I vowed that, if I had to have MS, by God I was going to do it well. This is a class act, ladies and gentlemen. No tears, no recriminations, no faint-heartedness.

One way and another, then, I wind up feeling like Tiny Tim, peering over the edge of the table at the Christmas goose, waving my crutch, piping down God's blessing on us all. Only sometimes I don't want to play Tiny Tim. I'd rather be Caliban, a most scurvy monster. Fortunately, at home no one much cares whether I'm a good cripple or a bad cripple as long as I make vichyssoise with fair regularity. One evening several years ago, Anne was reading at the dining-room table while I cooked dinner. As I opened a can of tomatoes, the can slipped in my left hand and juice spattered me and the counter with bloody spots. Fatigued and infuriated, I bellowed, "I'm so sick of being crippled!" Anne glanced at me over the top of her book. "There now," she said, "do you feel better?" "Yes," I said, "yes, I do." She went back to her reading. I felt better. That's about all the attention my scurviness ever gets.

20   Because I hate being crippled, I sometimes hate myself for being 20 a cripple. Over the years I have come to expect—even accept—attacks of violent self-loathing. Luckily, in general our society no longer connects deformity and disease directly with evil (though a charismatic once told me that I have MS because a devil is in me) and so I'm allowed to move largely at will, even among small children. But I'm not sure that this revision of attitude has been particularly helpful. Physical imperfection, even freed of moral disapprobation, still defies and violates the ideal, especially for women, whose confinement in their bodies as objects of desire is far from over. Each age, of course, has its ideal, and I doubt that ours is any better or worse than any other. Today's ideal woman, who lives on the glossy pages of dozens of magazines, seems to be between the ages of eighteen and twenty-five; her hair has body, her teeth flash white, her breath smells minty, her underarms are dry; she has a career but is still a fabulous cook, especially of meals that take less than twenty minutes to prepare; she does not ordinarily appear to have a husband or children; she is trim and deeply tanned; she jogs, swims, plays tennis, rides a bicycle, sails, but does not

bowl; she travels widely, even to out-of-the-way places like Finland and Samoa, always in the company of the ideal man, who possesses a nearly identical set of characteristics. There are a few exceptions. Though usually white and often blonde, she may be black, Hispanic, Asian, or Native American, so long as she is unusually sleek. She may be old, provided she is selling a laxative or is Lauren Bacall. If she is selling a detergent, she may be married and have a flock of strikingly messy children. But she is never a cripple.

Like many women I know, I have always had an uneasy relationship with my body. I was not a popular child, largely, I think now, because I was peculiar: intelligent, intense, moody, shy, given to unexpected actions and inexplicable notions and emotions. But as I entered adolescence, I believed myself unpopular because I was homely: my breasts too flat, my mouth too wide, my hips too narrow, my clothing never quite right in fit or style. I was not, in fact, particularly ugly, old photographs inform me, though I was well off the ideal; but I carried this sense of self-alienation with me into adulthood, where it regenerated in response to the depredations of MS. Even with my brace I walk with a limp so pronounced that, seeing myself on the videotape of a television program on the disabled, I couldn't believe that anything but an inchworm could make progress humping along like that. My shoulders droop and my pelvis thrusts forward as I try to balance myself upright, throwing my frame into a bony S. As a result of contractures, one shoulder is higher than the other and I carry one arm bent in front of me, the fingers curled into a claw. My left arm and leg have wasted into pipe-stems, and I try always to keep them covered. When I think about how my body must look to others, especially to men, to whom I have been trained to display myself, I feel ludicrous, even loathsome.

At my age, however, I don't spend much time thinking about my appearance. The burning egocentricity of adolescence, which assures one that all the world is looking all the time, has passed, thank God, and I'm generally too caught up in what I'm doing to step back, as I used to, and watch myself as though upon a stage. I'm also too old to believe in the accuracy of self-image. I know that I'm not a hideous crone, that in fact, when I'm rested, well dressed, and well made up, I look fine. The self-loathing I feel is neither physically nor intellectually substantial. What I hate is not me but a disease.

I am not a disease.

And a disease is not—at least not singlehandedly—going to determine who I am, though at first it seemed to be going to. Adjusting to a chronic incurable illness, I have moved through a process similar to that outlined by Elizabeth Kübler-Ross in *On Death and Dying*. The major difference—and it is far more significant than most people recognize—is that I can't be sure of the outcome, as the terminally ill cancer patient can. Research studies indicate that, with proper medical care, I may achieve a "normal" life span. And in our society, with its vision of death as the ultimate evil, worse even than decrepitude, the response to such news is, "Oh well, at least you're not going to *die*." Are there worse things than dying? I think that there may be.

25   I think of two women I know, both with MS, both enough older   25 than I to have served as models. One took to her bed several years ago and has been there ever since. Although she can sit in a high-backed wheelchair, because she is incontinent she refuses to go out at all, even though incontinence pants, which are readily available at any pharmacy, could protect her from embarrassment. Instead, she stays at home and insists that her husband, a small quiet man, a retired civil servant, stay there with her except for a quick weekly foray to the supermarket. The other woman, whose illness was diagnosed when she was eighteen, a nursing student engaged to a young doctor, finished her training, married her doctor, accompanied him to Germany when he was in the service, bore three sons and a daughter, now grown and gone. When she can, she travels with her husband; she plays bridge, embroiders, swims regularly; she works, like me, as a symptomatic-patient instructor of medical students in neurology. Guess which woman I hope to be.

At the beginning, I thought about having MS almost incessantly. And because of the unpredictable course of the disease, my thoughts were always terrified. Each night I'd get into bed wondering whether I'd get out again the next morning, whether I'd be able to see, to speak, to hold a pen between my fingers. Knowing that the day might come when I'd be physically incapable of killing myself, I thought perhaps I ought to do so right away, while I still had the strength. Gradually I came to understand that the Nancy who might one day lie inert under a bedsheet, arms and legs paralyzed, unable to feed or bathe herself, unable to reach out for a gun, a bottle of pills, was not the Nancy I was at present, and that I could not presume to make decisions for that future Nancy, who might well not want in the least to die. Now the only provision I've made for the future Nancy is that when the time comes—and it is likely to come in the form of pneumonia, friend to the weak and the old—I am not to be treated with machines and medications. If she is unable to communicate by then, I hope she will be satisfied with these terms.

Thinking all the time about having MS grew tiresome and intrusive, especially in the large and tragic mode in which I was accustomed to considering my plight. Months and even years went by without catastrophe (at least without one related to MS), and really I was awfully busy, what with George and children and snakes and students and poems, and I hadn't the time, let alone the inclination, to devote myself to being a disease. Too, the richer my life became, the funnier it seemed, as though there were some connection between largesse and laughter, and so my tragic stance began to waver until, even with the aid of a brace and cane, I couldn't hold it for very long at a time.

After several years I was satisfied with my adjustment. I had suffered my grief and fury and terror, I thought, but now I was at ease with my lot. Then one summer day I set out with George and the children across the desert for a vacation in California. Part way to Yuma I became aware that my right leg felt funny. "I think I've had an exacerbation," I told George. "What shall we do?" he asked. "I think we'd better get the hell to California," I said, "because I don't know whether I'll ever make it again." So we went on to San Diego and then to Orange, and up the Pacific Coast Highway to Santa Cruz, across to Yosemite, down to Sequoia and Joshua Tree, and so back over the desert to home. It was a fine two-week trip, filled with friends and fair weather, and I wouldn't have missed it for the world, though I did in fact make it back to California two years later. Nor would there have been any point in missing it, since in MS, once the symptoms have appeared, the neurological damage has been done, and there's no way to predict or prevent that damage.

The incident spoiled my self-satisfaction, however. It renewed my grief and fury and terror, and I learned that one never finishes adjusting to MS. I don't know now why I thought one would. One does not, after all, finish adjusting to life, and MS is simply a fact of my life—not my favorite fact, of course—but as ordinary as my nose and my tropical fish and my yellow Mazda station wagon. It may at any time get worse, but no amount of worry or anticipation can prepare me for a new loss. My life is a lesson in losses. I learn one at a time.

30 And I had best be patient in the learning, since I'll have to do it 30 like it or not. As any rock fan knows, you can't always get what you want. Particularly when you have MS. You can't, for example, get cured. In recent years researchers and the organizations that fund research have started to pay MS some attention even though it isn't fatal; perhaps they have begun to see that life is something other than a quantitative phenomenon, that one may be very much alive for a very long time in a life that isn't worth living. The researchers have made some progress toward understanding the mechanism of the disease: It may well be an autoimmune reaction triggered by a slow-acting virus. But they are nowhere near its prevention, control, or cure. And most of us want to be cured. Some, unable to accept incurability, grasp at one treatment after another, no matter how bizarre: megavitamin therapy, gluten-free diet, injections of cobra venom, hypothermal suits, lymphocytopharesis, hyperbaric chambers. Many treatments are probably harmless enough, but none are curative.

The absence of a cure often makes MS patients bitter toward their doctors. Doctors are, after all, the priests of modern society, the new shamans, whose business is to heal, and many an MS patient roves from one to another, searching for the "good" doctor who will make him well. Doctors too think of themselves as healers, and for this reason many have trouble dealing with MS patients, whose disease in its intransigence defeats their aims and mocks their skills. Too few doctors, it is true, treat their patients as whole human beings, but the reverse is also true. I have always tried to be gentle with my doctors, who often have more at stake in terms of ego than I do. I may be frustrated, maddened, depressed by the incurability of my disease, but I am not diminished by it, and they are. When I push myself up from my seat in the waiting room and stumble toward them, I incarnate the limitation of their powers. The least I can do is refuse to press on their tenderest spots.

This gentleness is part of the reason that I'm not sorry to be a cripple. I didn't have it before. Perhaps I'd have developed it anyway—how could I know such a thing?—and I wish I had more of it, but I'm glad of what I have. It has opened and enriched my life enormously, this sense that my frailty and need must be mirrored in others, that in searching for and shaping a stable core in a life wrenched by change and loss, change and loss, I must recognize the same process, under individual conditions, in the lives around me. I do not deprecate such knowledge, however I've come by it.

189

All the same, if a cure were found, would I take it? In a minute. I may be a cripple, but I'm only occasionally a loony and never a saint. Anyway, in my brand of theology God doesn't give bonus points for a limp. I'd take a cure; I just don't need one. A friend who also has MS startled me once by asking, "Do you ever say to yourself, 'Why me, Lord?' " "No, Michael, I don't," I told him, "because whenever I try, the only response I can think of is 'Why not?' " If I could make a cosmic deal, who would I put in my place? What in my life would I give up in exchange for sound limbs and a thrilling rush of energy? No one. Nothing. I might as well do the job myself. Now that I'm getting the hang of it.

Questions on Meaning

1. Why is Mairs so insistent on calling herself a cripple rather than disabled or a handicapped person?
2. At several different points in the essay Mairs writes about the need for a sense of humor. Explain what the essay shows about the relationship of illness and humor.
3. What does the essay say about the importance of friends and family? How does the essay apply this not only to the disabled but to everyone?

Questions on Rhetorical Strategy and Style

1. How is this essay structured? Can you find a discernible movement or development from the beginning to the end? Describe it.
2. In some ways the essay is a long attempt to define what it means to have multiple sclerosis. What strategies of definition does the author use?

Writing Assignments

1. Mairs describes the "ideal woman" seen in advertisements and comments. They are never crippled or otherwise less than perfect. Write an essay explaining why our society seems to have difficulty accepting images of disabled people.
2. Think about how you react when interacting with disabled persons you encounter in public situations. Do you avoid interaction, not wanting to encroach on the individual's independence, or do you offer assistance? Or something in between? How do you think your response is judged by most disabled people?
3. Mairs writes, "In our society, anyone who deviates from the norm had better find some way to compensate." In addition to having disabled people having to compensate for their condition, she comments that overweight people are expected to be jolly. How do you react to this generalization? Can you think of other examples of people expected to compensate for their differences?

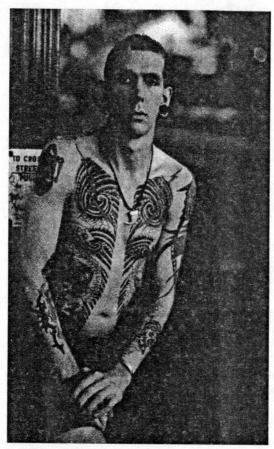

Steve McCurry, Tattooed man in Los Angeles (1991).

⚘ CHICKEN-HIPS* ⚘

Catherine Pigott

Catherine Pigott, producer for the Canadian Broadcasting Corporation's This Morning, *became aware of women's issues when she taught English in Gambia in the early 1980's. Since then she has continued to champion women's concerns, recently serving on the Advisory Committee to the Afghan Women's Organization and producing the 1998 Canadian project and report "Muslim Women in the Media." The idea for* Chicken Hips *occurred to Pigott after she watched Katherine Gilday's documentary on eating disorders entitled* The Famine Within. *Soon after an interview with Gilday, Pigott was moved to pen the following essay.*

1   The women of the household clucked disapprovingly when they saw me. It was the first time I had worn African clothes since my arrival in tiny, dusty Gambia, and evidently they were not impressed. They adjusted my head-tie and pulled my *lappa,* the ankle-length fabric I had wrapped around myself, even tighter. "You're too thin," one of them pronounced. "It's no good." They nicknamed me "Chicken-hips."

    I marvelled at this accolade, for I had never been called thin in my life. It was something I longed for. I would have been flattered if those ample-bosomed women hadn't looked so distressed. It was obvious I fell far short of their ideal of beauty.

    I had dressed up for a very special occasion—the baptism of a son. The women heaped rice into tin basins the size of laundry tubs, shaping it into mounds with their hands. Five of us sat around one basin, thrusting our fingers into the scalding food. These women ate with such relish, such joy. They pressed the rice into balls in their fists, squeezing until the bright-red palm oil ran down their forearms and dripped off their elbows.

I tried desperately, but I could not eat enough to please them. It was hard for me to explain that I come from a culture in which it is almost unseemly for a woman to eat too heartily. It's considered unattractive. It was even harder to explain that to me thin is beautiful, and in my country we deny ourselves food in our pursuit of perfect slenderness.

5   That night, everyone danced to welcome the baby. Women swivelled their broad hips and used their hands to emphasize the roundness of their bodies. One needed to be round and wide to make the dance beautiful. There was no place for thinness here. It made people sad. It reminded them of things they wanted to forget, such as poverty, drought and starvation. You never knew when the rice was going to run out.

I began to believe that Africa's image of the perfect female body was far more realistic than the long-legged leanness I had been conditioned to admire. There, it is beautiful—not shameful—to carry weight on the hips and thighs, to have a round stomach and heavy, swinging breasts. Women do not battle the bulge, they celebrate it. A body is not something to be tamed and moulded.

The friends who had christened me Chicken-hips made it their mission to fatten me up. It wasn't long before a diet of rice and rich, oily stew twice a day began to change me. Every month, the women would take a stick and measure my backside, noting with pleasure its gradual expansion. "Oh Catherine, your buttocks are getting nice now!" They would say.

What was extraordinary was that I, too, believed I was becoming more beautiful. There was no sense of panic, no shame, no guilt-ridden resolves to go on the miracle grape-and-water diet. One day, I tied my *lappa* tight across my hips and went to the market to buy beer for a wedding. I carried the crate of bottles home on my head, swinging my hips slowly as I walked. I felt transformed.

In Gambia, people don't use words such as "cheating," "naughty," or "guilty" when they talk about eating. The language of sin is not applied to food. Fat is desirable. It holds beneficial meanings of abundance, fertility and health.

10   My perception of beauty altered as my body did. The European tourists on the beach began to look strange and skeletal rather than

"slim." They had no hips. They seemed devoid of shape and substance. Women I once would have envied appeared fragile and even ugly. The ideal they represented no longer made sense.

After a year, I came home. I preached my new way of seeing to anyone who would listen. I wanted to cling to the liberating belief that losing weight had nothing to do with self-love.

Family members kindly suggested that I might look and feel better if I slimmed down a little. They encouraged me to join an exercise club. I wandered around the malls in a dislocated daze. I felt uncomfortable trying on clothes that hung so elegantly on the mannequins. I began hearing old voices inside my head: "Plaid makes you look fat. . . . You're too short for that style. . . . Vertical stripes are more slimming. . . . Wear black."

I joined the club. Just a few weeks after I had worn a *lappa* and scooped up rice with my hands, I was climbing into pink leotards and aerobics shoes. The instructor told me that I had to set fitness goals and "weigh in" after my workouts. There were mirrors on the walls and I could see women watching themselves. I sensed that even the loveliest among them felt they were somehow flawed. As the aerobics instructor barked out commands for arm lifts and leg lifts, I pictured Gambian women pounding millet and dancing in a circle with their arms raised high. I do not mean to romanticize their rock-hard lives, but we were hardly to be envied as we ran like fools between two walls to the tiresome beat of synthesized music.

We were a roomful of women striving to reshape ourselves into some kind of pubertal ideal. I reverted to my natural state: one of yearning to be slimmer and more fit than I was. My freedom had been temporary. I was home, where fat is feared and despised. It was time to exert control over my body and my life. I dreaded the thought of people saying, "She's let herself go."

15   If I return to Africa I am sure the women will shake their heads   15
in bewildered dismay. Even now, I sometimes catch my reflection in a window and their voices come back to me. "Yo! Chicken-hips!"

Questions on Meaning

1. Pigott tells the reader how it feels to have cultural assumptions questioned. How do the Gambian women make Pigott feel about herself?

2. Pigott says that she believed she was becoming more beautiful as she ate more. What does it mean to be beautiful? Who decides who is beautiful and who is not?

3. What happens to Pigott when she returns to Canada from Africa? Why does she conform to the starvation and exercise cult?

Questions on Strategy and Style

1. Pigott compares the attitudes of Gambian women to those of Canadian women. How does this comparison explain the point that the essay is making?

2. The descriptions of Gambian food are lush and vivid—red grease on balls of rice, for example. How do these descriptions affect the reader?

3. Pigott tells the story of her weight gain and loss. How do you feel about this story? What does it make you think about your own experiences with food?

Writing Assignments

1. Consider the term *chicken hips*. Does every North American woman want to have chicken hips? Take a survey of friends and acquaintances, if possible asking women who are not native to North America too. Write about the responses to your survey.

2. Look up Gambia on the Internet or in the library. Write about the country. What kinds of work do people do in Gambia? What kinds of lives do they lead? Contrast your findings with your own life.

3. Pigott assumes that North American attitudes toward food and beauty are skewed. Write about your own experiences with food identity. Do you think that North American values force young people, especially women, to be unhappy with themselves? Why?

VIRTUAL SEX, LIES AND CYBERSPACE

Amy Harmon

Amy Harmon (1968–) has an undergraduate degree in American culture from the University of Michigan. She now works as a reporter for the New York Times, *after having been a staff reporter for seven years at the* Los Angeles Times. *In this selection, Harmon writes about the world of online junkies and the fantasies that feed their addictions.*

1   The first time Donna Tancordo "cybered," she switched off her computer midway through the typed seduction, shocked and scared at the power of the words scrolling down her screen.

"I've never described what I was feeling like that before," she said. "I freaked out."

But Tancordo, a happily married New Jersey housewife with three kids, soon logged back onto America Online. In a chat room called "Married and Flirting," she met another man. For days, they whispered the details of their lives into the ether. When he asked her if he could take her on a virtual trip to the mountains, she agreed.

This time her computer stayed on.

5   All hours of the day and night, America Online's chat rooms teem with people seeking something missing in their lives—like Jay, a successful business consultant in Boston, who says he logs on to fill "the void of passionate emotion."

The blurted confidences and anonymous yearning scrolling through AOL's frames reveal a rare picture of the American psyche unshackled from social convention.

In the vacuum of cyberspace, self-exploration is secret and strangely safe. Much has been made lately of how cults may find fertile recruiting ground among online seekers. A vast range of support groups—for pregnant mothers, cancer patients, substance abusers—also flourish. Unlikely friendships are struck and sometimes sustained.

But in an age when sex is scary and intimacy scarce, the keyboard and modem perhaps most often serve a pressing quest for romantic connection and sexual discovery.

Eric lives in a small California farming town: "I'm pretty much a straight kind of dude." When he flips on the computer at 4:30 a.m. to check the weather, he is drawn to rooms where San Franciscans recount stories of sexual bondage.

10   Eleanor, 13, is 5-foot-1, with dark brown hair. When she surfs the   10
"Teen Chat" rooms after school, she looks for kicks as a tall strawberry blond.

Peter, a 45-year-old professional in Manhattan, spent his first weekend on AOL posing as a 26-year-old woman while his wife was away on business. Enthralled with the ease of uninhibited communion, he cycled through a whirl of identities. He disguised himself as a gay man, a lesbian and a young girl. But eventually he settled on a more mundane form of seduction.

"What I really wanted was to have sexual conversations with women," Peter said. "Kind of garden variety, but that's who I am, and what made it such a fever for me—that's not too strong a word—was the flirtation aspect of it."

The ritual of pursuing secret desires from behind a facade is as old as the masquerade. But perhaps because it has never been so easy, the compulsion has never seemed so strong.

"Leave the Meat Behind"

The free computer disks that arrive unbidden in the mail offer not only a mask, but an escape from the body—the ability, as cyberpunk author William Gibson puts it, to "leave the meat behind."

15   It is an offer with remarkable mass appeal. As AOLs subscriber   15
count doubled over the last year to 8 million, the number of chat rooms on busy nights tripled to 15,000. And the recent, much-publicized agitation over the service's busy signals was due

largely to people chatting longer, now that a new pricing plan means they do not have to pay by the minute.

AOL is by far the most popular gathering spot on the Internet, in part because its culture of anonymity—members can choose up to five fictional screen names—promotes what one observer calls "the online equivalent of getting drunk and making a fool of yourself." Although it is possible to chat on the World Wide Web and other areas of the Internet, the technology doesn't work nearly as well.

Largely because of the unabashed sexual character of many of its chat rooms, AOL executives traditionally have downplayed their importance to the company's bottom line. "What we're offering at AOL is convenience in a box," said AOL Network's President Robert Pittman. "If you use AOL it will save you time. People aren't buying it for chat."

Perhaps. The service offers e-mail, Internet access and information and entertainment features. Many of its customers never venture near the chat rooms, and most usage of the Internet is unrelated to chat.

But according to America Online statistics, more than three-quarters of its subscribers use chat rooms at least once a month, the equivalent of 1 million hours a day

20 "If AOL eliminated chat you'd see the subscriber base go from 8 20 million to 1 million faster than you could spit," said Alan Weiner, an analyst at Dataquest, a consulting firm.

Not all chat is laden with sexual innuendo. "I can say I'm a voluptuous teen and I still don't get attention when I go into the sports and finance rooms," quipped one frequent female chatter.

Some chat rooms emerge as genuine communities where the same group gathers regularly. The "SoCalifover30" room even holds regular "fleshmeets" at restaurants or members' homes. A core group keeps up on one another's romantic exploits online and offline.

"Ladykuu," a San Diego bus driver trainer and the mother of twins, says she has become close friends with another mother of twins in Boston, with whom she shares life's tribulations.

But even Ladykuu enjoys "lurking" and listening to others tell secrets to which she ordinarily would not be privy:

25 "It's just fascinating to me to see, what is that deep dark fantasy 25 what is the naughty thing you're thinking about and—oh my gosh, I've been thinking about that too."

Some sexual-oriented chat is basic singles bar sleaze—and some is mainly an excuse to swap pornographic pictures. But much more prevalent is the search for genuine connection, and perhaps seduction.

Some chatters seek a companion to meet in person. Others, who shun the idea of a real-life affair, seize on the opportunity to engage in the thrill of a new seduction over the computer from the comfort of home—often while their spouses sleep in the next room.

Whether the demi-realities of chat can fulfill real world needs or only add to their urgency is a subject of much debate among online seekers. Some discover hidden pieces of themselves that lead to significant changes in what, in a telling delineation, is called RL—real life.

Others grow sickened by the relentless layering of illusion, where friends and lovers appear suddenly, and then melt into air, or morph into aliens. For there is in all this a bitter irony: That a search for intimacy brings people to pose as airbrushed versions of themselves, so that they may share their inner fantasies with strangers.

30 "It's not healthy for people to pretend to be someone they're not and fantasize about that constantly," said Nancy Wesson, a psychologist in Mountain View, California. She has seen marriages break up in part because of one partner's online activities. "It allows you to perpetually live in a fantasy instead of living in real life."

Ultimately, marriage may be the institution most rocked by the new technology. Although cyberspace obviously doesn't invent secret longings, it does provide a way to uncover and exploit them that has never been so available to so many

Cheating Without Really Cheating

Some flirters say the ability to cheat without really cheating, to voice fantasies somehow too personal to share even with spouses, has invigorated them.

Donna and Ralph Tancordo, high school sweethearts who have been married for 17 years, sign onto AOL and "cyber" with other married people—with each other's consent.

"My cheekbones hurt I've been smiling so much lately," said Donna, who opened her account a month ago. "I think it's the flattery. It's like, 'Wow, somebody else is attracted to me other than my husband.' And it's improved our sex life 150%."

35   In the case of Peter, the Manhattan professional, the online habit 35
nearly broke up his marriage. Finding a woman that he would care to
talk to and who would talk to him could take hours on any given
night. He would stay up after his wife, Janet, went to bed, and look
forward to when she would leave him alone at home.

In the end, Janet became too distraught over his regular online
meetings with a woman who lived thousands of miles away. Peter
agreed to cancel his AOL account. Both say the experience has opened
up a productive, if painful, period of exploration for them.

"I was bored and I lied about it to myself," Peter said. "I had a sex
life, but it didn't have passion. At some level, that's what I was seeking,
and it's hard to find. There may not be an answer."

For Janet, the hardest part has been trying to sift out what may
be her husband's harmless fantasy life from what to her is hurtful
reality.

"Everyone knows someone who has had an affair," Janet said. "If
your husband's having an affair and you tell your girlfriend, you're
going to have instant sympathy. But do I have a right to be pissed
about this? I don't know."

40   She has not talked to any of her friends about it: "It's 40
embarrassing. I don't know anyone else who has gone through this."

A lot of people have. The online consensus is that, as Tiffany
Cook of the SoCalifover30 chat room puts it, "if you're talking to a
married man often enough, that's an affair even if you never meet."

But in the 1990s, when interest in family values is on the rise and
the ethic of safe sex prevails, AOL offers 1960s-style free love from
behind the safety of the screen. The medium offers a sense of physical
and psychological safety that strips away taboos faster than the sexual
revolution ever did.

Many married people—they constitute two-thirds of AOL
subscribers—comb chat rooms, scope the profiles and send private
instant messages (IMs) to prospective romantic partners.

The flirtation medium of choice, IMs pop up on-screen as soon
as they are sent, heedless of whatever the recipient may be doing.
More insistent and perhaps more intimate than e-mail, they solicit an
immediate response.

45   "I've tried erotic e-mail. It's like bad D. H. Lawrence," said an 45
artist who prefers the edge of IMs.

Three million IM sessions are opened every day. They are by nature fleeting and the exchange is rapid-fire, lessening the risk and increasing the nerve.

"I make advances to men the same age group as I am to start flirting and sometimes it goes a lot further than flirt," said Donna. "I read their profile first. If I like it, I'll IM them by saying . . . 'BUSY?'"

In the curious state of disembodiment, where the body is nonetheless very much the point, the typed words come as stream of consciousness, and then, with the click of a mouse, they disappear.

"I'm sorry I can't talk right now," one woman tells a reporter. "I'm getting nine IMs as we speak."

50   Often, IM exchanges begin between people in the same chat room. At any given moment, subscribers fill rooms of varying salaciousness—"Hot and Ready Female," "Discreet in Illinois," "CA Cops Who Flirt," "BiCuriousM4M." Many of the chat rooms created by subscribers—as opposed to those established by AOL—have overtly sexual themes and many others draw people interested in romance.

"There's a lot more diversity out there than I would have given people credit for," said Jenny, a 27-year-old lesbian from Manhattan who roams the chat rooms when she is not using the service to check stock quotes.

"Wanna cyber?" comes the standard query, proffering the on-line equivalent of a one-night stand. "M/F?" "What are you wearing?"

"On AOL you could be talking about sex within three minutes of meeting someone," said a 28-year-old male marketing consultant who goes by the handle "MindUnit."

Many simply want to experiment in the intricate art of flirtation, 55 sometimes behind a guise, sometimes as themselves.

"It's the only place you can throw yourself at someone and not care if you get rejected," said Jenny.

Women especially say the ability to both be more aggressive than they would in real life and to hit "cancel" or "ignore" if a flirtation gets out of control is liberating—and perhaps good practice.

For many, the point is not cybersex per se, but delving into the forbidden realm of sexuality. Says one online explorer on the East Coast: "We live in a world and particularly this culture that seeks to, on the surface, completely repress our sexuality. I think for many people, AOL represents a safe and healthy expression, although, like all pleasures, from fatty foods to erotic pleasure, there is probably a price to pay."

After empty nights of chat room prowling for the ideal cybermate, many end up being as disappointing as such searches often are in real life.

"All I can tell you is that there are thousands of searching people out there . . . and AOL has become a vehicle to meet others . . . affairs, etc. . . . ." types a Southern California man to a reporter one Saturday night. "But it doesn't solve the problems of real life."

60 Sometimes connections that seem solid suddenly fade away. Even carefree Donna was thrown off-balance recently when her AOL lover sent a cryptic message saying he wouldn't be spending as much time online.

"He was basically blowing me off and I was really upset," she said. "I was sitting in the dentist's chair and I couldn't get him out of my head. I've gotten too emotional about this. I really need to handle it better."

Psychologists caution against getting wrapped up in a reality that is not, in fact, real. And online junkies acknowledge that it can be hard to pull out of what one calls "AOL's sticky web," which can become an addictive escape from three-dimensional existence.

Psychologist Kimberly Young, who has studied online addiction, says it's comparable to compulsive gambling in its mood-altering appeal—and is just as dangerous.

Sherry Turkle, a professor of the sociology of science at the Massachusetts Institute of Technology, draws a more optimistic conclusion. In her recent book, *Life on the Screen,* she argues that online technology is enabling a new, decentered sense of identity to emerge, and that the practice of trying on different personalities could be a useful way to work through real-life issues.

65 Swapping genders is a popular activity among both sexes, but since (real) men outnumber women by about 2 to 1, the likelihood of talking to a man claiming to be a woman is fairly high.

MindUnit has devised an only-sort-of tongue-in-cheek "Rules to Establish Gender," testament that even in a world without gender, well-socialized roles remain largely intact.

They state, in part: "If she sounds 'too good to be true,' that is One Strike. If she has no profile, that is One Strike. If she seems preoccupied with sex, or starts the sex talk herself, that is One Strike.

If she volunteers exact statistics about herself, especially measurements or bra size, that is One Strike. If the statistics are really hot, that is Two Strikes." By MindUnit's trauma-tested logic, three strikes means the woman you're chatting with is a man.

Little in the AOL chat world is as it appears to be. But, for many, the chance to honestly express their desires and be privy to those of others outweighs the veil of lies that seems somehow necessary to make it possible. "Let me find someone with an open mind, good intentions, and sincerity," reads MindUnit's profile. "Failing that, I'll take a nymphomaniac."

Few know better than Tiffany Cook the perils of confusing online illusions with real-life truths. First, the 30-year-old Santa Monica interior designer hit it off with a man who flew to visit her from New York. The chemistry didn't translate in person.

But then for three months she spent hours a day chatting with a man from Northern California. He said he was 33. Then he confessed to being 43, and then to his actual age: 71. He had sent her a picture—it turned out to be of his son.

"It was terrible," she said. "I felt so deceived."

Still, Tiffany, who changed her screen name after learning the truth about her most passionate correspondence, still spends part of almost every day online.

"You know what? It's expanded my world," she said. "I've laughed really hard and I've learned a lot, and no matter what I might think of [him] now, the fact is we had a huge amount to talk about.

"Besides, your chances of meeting someone who's hiding behind something online and someone who's hiding behind something in real life [are] about the same."

Questions on Meaning

1. Harmon's piece deals with a growing trend: online addiction. According to Harmon, what has led to this development? What are some of its consequences of it? Are there any positive aspects to online culture? If so, what are they?
2. How are online conversations different from face-to-face exchanges? What changes in social habits and arrangements do they cause?
3. Does Harmon suggest that women are more likely to become online junkies than men? If so, do you agree or disagree? Is the same true for teen girls and boys? If so, what does this imply about gender or other identity issues?

Questions on Rhetorical Strategy and Style

1. Most of the information in this report comes from personal accounts. Do you see these accounts as representative of people in general? Why or why not? How effective are these accounts, in your view? What do you find most convincing about the selection? What makes you skeptical?
2. Any piece of writing has an angle and reflects the writer's attitude. Demonstrate how Harmon tries to remain unbiased in the selection. What overall point of view emerges from what she presents and how she presents it?

Writing Assignments

1. Visit a popular online chat room and analyze it the way a cultural anthropologist might. That is, try to understand how that "society" is arranged. Which members get to nominate topics, and what do they talk about? If so, what appears to be important to the participants? Are there any power struggles? If so, how would you characterize them? What kinds of identities are members presenting online?
2. Write an opinion piece about online culture. Explore questions such as the following: Why are online relationships so popular today? How has human interaction changed because of this technology? What have we gained? What have we lost?

THE ANDROGYNOUS MAN

Noel Perrin

Noel Perrin (1927–), has pursued a wide variety of interests. He has taught as a professor of English and environmental studies at Dartmouth, farmed in Vermont, contributed articles and columns to high culture periodicals such as The New Yorker *and* The Washington Post, *and written a series of books in which he meditates on culture and art:* A Passport Secretly Green; *(1961);* First Person Rural: More Essays of a Sometime Farmer *(1981);* Last Person Rural *(1991); and* Solo: Life with an Electric Cat *(1992). In the essay that follows, Perrin criticizes the stereotypical role of the American male, suggesting an alternate, more feminized role that may be healthier.*

1   The summer I was 16, I took a train from New York to Steamboat Springs, Colo., where I was going to be assistant horse wrangler at a camp. The trip took three days, and since I was much too shy to talk to strangers, I had quite a lot of time for reading. I read all of "Gone With the Wind." I read all the interesting articles in a couple of magazines I had, and then I went back and read all the dull stuff. I also took all the quizzes, a thing of which magazines were even fuller then than now.

The one that held my undivided attention was called "How Masculine/Feminine Are You?" It consisted of a large number of inkblots. The reader was supposed to decide which of four objects each blot most resembled. The choices might be a cloud, a steam engine, a caterpillar and a sofa.

When I finished the test, I was shocked to find that I was barely masculine at all. On a scale of 1 to 10, I was about 1.2. Me, the horse

---

From *The New York Times Magazine* (February 5, 1984). Published by The New York Times. Copyright © 1984 by The New York Times Company.

wrangler? (And not just wrangler, either. That summer, I had to skin a couple of horses that died—the camp owner wanted the hides.)

The results of that test were so terrifying to me that for the first time in my life I did a piece of original analysis. Having unlimited time on the train, I looked at the "masculine" answers over and over, trying to find what it was that distinguished real men from people like me—and eventually I discovered two very simple patterns. It was "masculine" to think the blots looked like man-made objects, and "feminine" to think they looked like natural objects. It was masculine to think they looked like things capable of causing harm, and feminine to think of innocent things.

Even at 16, I had the sense to see that the compilers of the test were using rather limited criteria—maleness and femaleness are both more complicated than *that*—and I breathed a huge sigh of relief. I wasn't necessarily a wimp, after all.

That the test did reveal something other than the superficiality of its makers I realized only many years later. What it revealed was that there is a large class of men and women both, to which I belong, who are essentially androgynous. That doesn't mean we're gay, or low in the appropriate hormones, or uncomfortable performing the jobs traditionally assigned our sexes. (A few years after that summer, I was leading troops in combat and, unfashionable as it now is to admit this, having a very good time. War is exciting. What a pity the 20th century went and spoiled it with high-tech weapons.)

What it does mean to be spiritually androgynous is a kind of freedom. Men who are all-male, or he-man, or 100 percent red-blooded Americans, have a little biological set that causes them to be attracted to physical power, and probably also to dominance. Maybe even to watching football. I don't say this to criticize them. Completely masculine men are quite often wonderful people: good husbands, good (though sometimes overwhelming) fathers, good members of society. Furthermore, they are often so unself-consciously at ease in the world that other men seek to imitate them. They just aren't as free as us androgynes. They pretty nearly have to be what they are; we have a range of choices open.

The sad part is that many of us never discover that. Men who are not 100 percent red-blooded Americans—say, those who are only 75 percent red-blooded—often fail to notice their freedom. They are too busy trying to copy the he-men ever to realize that men, like women, come in a wide variety of acceptable types. Why this frantic imitation? My answer is mere speculation, but not casual. I have speculated on this for a long time.

Partly they're just envious of the he-man's unconscious ease. Mostly they're terrified of finding that there may be something wrong with them deep down, some weakness at the heart. To avoid discovering that, they spend their lives acting out the role that the he-man naturally lives. Sad.

10   One thing that men owe to the women's movement is that this kind of failure is less common than it used to be. In releasing themselves from the single ideal of the dependent woman, women have more or less incidentally released a lot of men from the single ideal of the dominant male. The one mistake the feminists have made, I think, is in supposing that *all* men need this release, or that the world would be a better place if all men achieved it. It wouldn't. It would just be duller.

So far I have been pretty vague about just what the freedom of the androgynous man is. Obviously it varies with the case. In the case I know best, my own, I can be quite specific. It has freed me most as a parent. I am, among other things, a fairly good natural mother. I like the nurturing role. It makes me feel good to see a child eat—and it turns me to mush to see a 4-year-old holding a glass with both small hands, in order to drink. I even enjoyed sewing patches on the knees of my daughter Amy's Dr. Dentons when she was at the crawling stage. All that pleasure I would have lost if I had made myself stick to the notion of the paternal role that I started with.

Or take a smaller and rather ridiculous example. I feel free to kiss cats. Until recently it never occurred to me that I would want to, though my daughters have been doing it all their lives. But my elder daughter is now 22, and in London. Of course, I get to look after her cat while she is gone. He's a big, handsome farm cat named Petrushka, very unsentimental, though used from kittenhood to being kissed on the top of the head by Elizabeth. I've gotten very fond of him (he's the adventurous kind of cat who likes to climb hills with you), and one night I simply felt like kissing him on the top of the head, and did. Why did no one tell me sooner how silky cat fur is?

Then there's my relation to cars. I am completely unembarrassed by my inability to diagnose even minor problems in whatever object

I happen to be driving, and don't have to make some insider's remark to mechanics to try to establish that I, too, am a "Man With His Machine."

The same ease extends to household maintenance. I do it, of course. Service people are expensive. But for the last decade my house has functioned better than it used to because I've had the aid of a volume called "Home Repairs Any Woman Can Do," which is pitched just right for people at my technical level. As a youth, I'd as soon have touched such a book as I would have become a transvestite. Even though common sense says there is really nothing sexual whatsoever about fixing sinks.

15   Or take public emotion. All my life I have easily been moved by   15 certain kinds of voices. The actress Siobhan McKenna's, to take a notable case. Give her an emotional scene in a play, and within 10 words my eyes are full of tears. In boyhood, my great dread was that someone might notice. I struggled manfully, you might say, to suppress this weakness. Now, of course, I don't see it as a weakness at all, but as a kind of fulfillment. I even suspect that the true he-men feel the same way, or one kind of them does, at least, and it's only the poor imitators who have to struggle to repress themselves.

Let me come back to the inkblots, with their assumption that masculine equates with machinery and science, and feminine with art and nature. I have no idea whether the right pronoun for God is He, She or It. But this I'm pretty sure of. If God could somehow be induced to take that test, God would not come out macho, and not feminismo, either, but right in the middle. Fellow androgynes, it's a nice thought.

Questions on Meaning

1. What qualities typify the macho man? The androgynous man?
2. Does Perrin seem defensive about his personal differences from the macho role? Identify and cite passages that support your answer.

Questions on Rhetorical Strategy and Style

1. Perrin uses comparison and examples to develop his argument about the androgynous man. Which form of development do you find more persuasive? Explain.
2. Perrin uses a style that might be termed "conversational." Think about how ordinary conversation differs from formal writing, list some of those differences, and locate examples of both conversational and formal style in Perrin's essay. Why do you think he uses this style?

Writing Assignments

1. Write an essay in which you describe the androgynous woman, or the child-adult, or the poor rich person, or some other compound of conventional social categories.
2. Write an essay defending the stereotypical macho man against the criticisms of androgynous and feminist critics. Imitate Perrin's low-key, non-confrontational style so that someone who disagreed with you could read the essay without feeling offended.

THE VEIL

Marjane Satrapi

Reprinted from *Persepolis: The Story of a Childhood,* edited by Mattias Ripa and Black Ferris (2003), Pantheon Books, a division of Random House.

AND ALSO BECAUSE THE YEAR BEFORE, IN 1979, WE WERE IN A FRENCH NON-RELIGIOUS SCHOOL.

WHERE BOYS AND GIRLS WERE TOGETHER

AND THEN SUDDENLY IN 1980...

ALL BILINGUAL SCHOOLS MUST BE CLOSED DOWN.

THEY ARE SYMBOLS OF CAPITALISM.

BRAVO!

WHAT WISDOM!

OF DECADENCE.

THIS IS CALLED A "CULTURAL REVOLUTION."

WE FOUND OURSELVES VEILED AND SEPARATED FROM OUR FRIENDS.

AND THAT WAS THAT...

EVERYWHERE IN THE STREETS THERE WERE DEMONSTRATIONS FOR AND AGAINST THE VEIL.

the veil! the veil! the veil! the veil! the veil! freedom! freedom! freedom! freedom! freedom!

AT ONE OF THE DEMONSTRATIONS, A GERMAN JOURNALIST TOOK A PHOTO OF MY MOTHER.

I WAS REALLY PROUD OF HER. HER PHOTO WAS PUBLISHED IN ALL THE EUROPEAN NEWSPAPERS.

AND EVEN IN ONE MAGAZINE IN IRAN. MY MOTHER WAS REALLY SCARED.

HAVE YOU SEEN THIS?

DON'T WORRY, DARLING.

SHE DYED HER HAIR,

AND WORE DARK GLASSES FOR A LONG TIME.

I REALLY DIDN'T KNOW WHAT TO THINK ABOUT THE VEIL. DEEP DOWN I WAS VERY RELIGIOUS BUT AS A FAMILY WE WERE VERY MODERN AND AVANT-GARDE.

I WAS BORN WITH RELIGION.

AT THE AGE OF SIX I WAS ALREADY SURE I WAS THE LAST PROPHET. THIS WAS A FEW YEARS BEFORE THE REVOLUTION.

O' Celestial light!

BEFORE ME THERE HAD BEEN A FEW OTHERS.

A WOMAN?

I AM THE LAST PROPHET.

I WANTED TO BE A PROPHET...

BECAUSE OUR MAID DID NOT EAT WITH US.

BECAUSE MY FATHER HAD A CADILLAC.

AND, ABOVE ALL, BECAUSE MY GRANDMOTHER'S KNEES ALWAYS ACHED.

COME HERE MARJI! HELP ME TO STAND UP.

DON'T WORRY, SOON YOU WON'T HAVE ANY MORE PAIN. YOU'LL SEE.

LIKE ALL MY PREDECESSORS I HAD MY HOLY BOOK.

THE FIRST THREE RULES CAME FROM ZARATHUSTRA. HE WAS THE FIRST PROPHET IN MY COUNTRY BEFORE THE ARAB INVASION.

YOU MUST BASE EVERYTHING ON THESE THREE RULES: BEHAVE WELL, SPEAK WELL, ACT WELL.

I ALSO WANTED US TO CELEBRATE THE TRADITIONAL ZARATHUSTRIAN HOLIDAYS. LIKE THE FIRE CEREMONY,

BEFORE THE PERSIAN NEW YEAR, NOROUZ, ON MARCH 21ST, THE FIRST DAY OF SPRING.

ONLY MY GRANDMOTHER KNEW ABOUT MY BOOK.

RULE NUMBER SIX: EVERYBODY SHOULD HAVE A CAR.

RULE NUMBER SEVEN: ALL MAIDS SHOULD EAT AT THE TABLE WITH THE OTHERS.

RULE NUMBER EIGHT: NO OLD PERSON SHOULD HAVE TO SUFFER.

IN THAT CASE, I'LL BE YOUR FIRST DISCIPLE.

REALLY?

BUT TELL ME HOW YOU'LL ARRANGE FOR OLD PEOPLE NOT TO SUFFER?

IT WILL SIMPLY BE FORBIDDEN.

Questions

1. How would you describe the style of drawing? Does it look sophisticated and elegant to you, or more like the work of a child? Do the drawings show a lot of detail, or do they give you a general idea of how people and places looked? Can you tell people apart?

2. How would you describe the style of writing? It is sophisticated and elegant, incredibly detailed, or . . . ?

3. Given the three categories of how words and drawings can interact (which we described in chapter 9), how would you say the words and drawings are interacting here? Could the words exist alone, and still have the same effect?

4. Why might Satrapi choose to start with a panel of herself, alone, at 10? What sort of *ethos* does this start to establish? What kind of *pathos* is being developed?

5. By the end of this first page, what conception of Iran has Satrapi constructed for her readers?

6. Notice how some of the panels have white backgrounds, and some black. What is going on in the panels with the black backgrounds? Why do you think Satrapi chose to use the black backgrounds where she has?

7. Why might Satrapi choose to show us the man's face in this row of panels first from close up, then from a distance, and then extremely close up?

8. You've read far enough to have a sense of the tone of voice in the writing. Is it highly emotional, or completely neutral, or . . . ? How does Satrapi show us emotion in this strip? Why might she have chosen to show emotion as she does?

9. Why do you think the drawing in the panel showing Satrapi's mother dyeing her hair is at an angle?

10. Why do you think Satrapi tells us about her own religious feelings several pages into her story, rather than at the very beginning?

11. How does Satrai represent the tensions she was feeling at the time? How do you understand those tensions?